Minimalism and Decluttering

Discover the secrets on How to live a meaningful life and Declutter your Home, Budget, Mind and Life with the Minimalist way of living

By

Alexandra Jessen

© **Copyright 2019 Alexandra Jessen, Minimalism and Decluttering - All rights reserved.**

In no way is it legal to reproduce, duplicate, or transmit any part of this document in either electronic means or in printed format. Recording of this publication is strictly prohibited and any storage of this document is not allowed unless with written permission from the author. All rights reserved.

Table of Contents

MINIMALISM 5

INTRODUCTION 7

DEFINITION OF MINIMALISM 10

HOW MINIMALISM IMPACTS
PEOPLE 12

HOW CAN MINIMALISM CHANGE
SOCIETY? 17

WAYS TO LIVE A HEALTHIER
LIFESTYLE 19

THE KEY ASPECTS TO MINIMALISM 30

PRACTICAL WAYS TO SIMPLIFY
YOUR LIFE 33

STEPS TO A MINIMALIST LIFESTYLE 42

SIMPLE WAYS TO SAVE MONEY 65

DIFFERENT LEVELS OF MINIMALISM 80

WHAT IS THE DOWNSIDE OF
MINIMALISM? 85

THE MISTAKES OF MINIMALISM 89

CORE PRINCIPLES TO MAXIMIZE LIVING AND LIVE ON PURPOSE 102

SIMPLICITY OF MINDFULNESS AND MEDITATION 111

30-DAY MINIMALISM CHALLENGE 118

TIPS TO DECLUTTER YOUR HOME 126

DECLUTTERING: PRACTICAL STEPS FOR LIVING WITH LESS 129

TECHNIQUES FOR PRACTICAL DECLUTTERING 133

HOW TO START DECLUTTERING YOUR LIFE: 5 SIMPLE STEPS 139

HERE'S HOW TO MAKE MINIMALISM WORK FOR YOU 143

CONCLUSION 147

ALEXANDRA JESSEN

MINIMALISM

As someone who has tried absolutely everything in the pursuit of happiness and the peace we all long for, I realized it can't be found in the latest iPhone or the 100 room mansion, while these things can be amazing and fun, they won't lead to lasting happiness. But, even more than that is all the meaningless 'stuff' we have collected and consumed over the years actually weighs us down and with it drags down our mood and can make us feel heavy. One day, it simply became too much for me and I took a stand, I decided to declutter my house and get rid of anything that didn't serve a purpose or provide me with enjoyment, happiness or joy I decided to get rid of it. This didn't mean I got rid of all my possessions, instead it was the start of a life long journey towards basing my life on what I love and find meaningful.

I will never be someone who lives in a box with 3 possessions to their name, however, I have learned that living in a way that serves you and actually leaves you feeling fulfilled and happy in every moment. No longer am I trying to find myself through the constant objects how I used to. And, what I have decided to do is to share and help as many people live in a way that makes them as happy as they can be.

MINIMALISM AND DECLUTTERING

There are no rules to this form of minimalism, everyone is different and that's what makes us human, but please approach all of these works by me as works that are only attempting to help you as much as I can from my own experience and years of research into what makes humans happy and joyful.

It's time we started focusing on what matters, and living life in a way that we love, that is meaningful and that fills us up with fulfillment, and I hope I can help you on your Journey.

All the best,

Alexandra

ALEXANDRA JESSEN

INTRODUCTION

If you're reading this eBook, chances are you're keen on decluttering and leaving on the adventure of a progressively minimalist lifestyle. Maybe this is your first enthusiastic, splendid peered toward attack into the universe of minimalism and you're searching for some basic tips to begin, or maybe you've figured out how to heave yourself back on the wagon after one more fizzled endeavor and are presently frantic for some motivation. Regardless of what your conditions, I am here to help with all the tips, traps and inspiration you need to set your minimalist objectives and stick to them!

Minimalism, like most other "- ism" developments, has unjustifiably turned into an object of criticism and, some of the time, by and large disdain, rejected as a hippy craze unlikely to stand the trial of time. Although these contentions may urge you to solidly walk out on minimalism (or run shouting for the slopes, if you're inclined to showy behavior), it's significant that numerous individuals harbor these feelings under the confused assumption that a noteworthy life change is basic to minimalism.

MINIMALISM AND DECLUTTERING

When we burrow a little more profound it turns out to be evident that, notwithstanding what you may have heard, minimalism just isn't tied in with living out of a cardboard box or segregating yourself from life's little pleasures or even quickly cutting back your 4 room cottage to a smallish lodge. Or maybe, the minimalist development essentially looks to perceive the overabundances of day by day life and prune them back to a progressively sensible dimension. In this sense, minimalism isn't tied in with denying ourselves, but rather about disposing of the extravagances we don't want so we have additional time and assets to focus on the things that really matter.

Removing clutter prepares for a life focused on the things that issue most. It opens up physical space in our home and mental space in our psyche. Living clutter free offers potential for more focus, more opportunity, passion and purposefulness. It diminishes pressure and money related commitments. Surprisingly better, expelling the physical clutter from our home establishes a foundation that makes significant life changes conceivable. It urges us to address assumptions and welcomes insightful thought of all aspects of our lives.

In this book, You will discover attentive and useful ideas on spring cleaning, dispersing your storeroom, and decluttering your psyche. This issue also addresses vital generational issues, for example, how to assist your maturing guardians in cutting back their homes and how to show youthful kids to declutter their rooms.

You don't need to be effectively carrying on with a Minimalist life to appreciate this book. This book is for any individual who's not totally content with their present life. Question is that being cheerful and investigates how to carry on with an important life. If you can peruse this book with a receptive outlook you might have the capacity to make a stride back and take stock of your present life, you may find that specific things you are doing or things that you possess are hindering your very own joy or opportunity.

DEFINITION OF MINIMALISM

Minimalism is a development in art, move, music, and so forth. Starting during the 1960s, in which just the simple designs, structures, forms, and so on are used, frequently redundantly, and the art's uniqueness is limited.

If you have chosen to live with less, you may have also considered about minimalism. Finding out about modern day minimalists and people, living less complex livesmay have you confused about what minimalism really is. How can all of these people be minimalists, when their lives are so dissimilar?

It is marked by clarity, reason, and purposefulness. At its focus, minimalism isthe purposeful advancement of the things we most value and the expulsion of everything that diverts us from it.It is life that powers purposely. Thus, it powers enhancements in all aspects of your life.

Toward the starting, you may characterize minimalism as wiping out your refuse cabinet. When you begin to unclutter, you quickly observe the advantages of living with less.

This benefit may be something as simple as always being able to find that one thing you used to spend time looking for. As you start to enjoy the advantage, you search for tactics to live more simply. What begins as an outside voyage (giving things away, cutting the link), turns out to be extremely personal, purposeful and more important. You begin to consider "stuff" things as well as commitment, debt and stress. Then, you perceive how this "stuff" is hindering your LIFE and choose to roll out a greater improvement. It's now that minimalism becomes more about who you are, rather than what you have.

Just, minimalism is:

- Ultimate simplicity
- Working towards genuine freedom
- Redefining freedom
- Expecting and receiving change
- Living with less
- The reply to "that's it"
- Making time and space to find what is really significant
- Spending additional time with people who lift me up and lifting them right back

HOW MINIMALISM IMPACTS PEOPLE

Whether you consider minimalism to be a philosophy, a truth or a guiding principle, its effects depend completely on what you decide to pursue.

As indicated by Joshua Becker, a key idea pioneer of the present minimalism development, minimalism is the deliberate advancement of the things we most value and the removal of everything that distract us from it.

So if the thing we most value is to love life, accomplish our own and professional objectives, and go on the most epic vacation, that is the thing that minimalism will assist us with doing.

But if the thing we most value includes having our very own effect outside lives, at that point minimalism will allow us to do that.

Minimalism Asks Life's Most Important Question.

ALEXANDRA JESSEN

I think what I cherish most about minimalism is that it drives us to confront ourselves. No more holing up behind purchases, behind accomplishments, or behind busy ness. We need to make sense of the response to the questions, what really matters most to me. I love that minimalism doesn't answer that question for us; we need to.

Minimalism Cultivates Self-Control.

As we become more thoughtful about what is on our notorious plate– from the things in our homes to the responsibilities in our timetables to the things on our to-do list– we figure out how to lean far from the driving forces that instigate the abundance in the first place.We start to shift from "What do I want at this moment?" to "What is the best decision here long haul?"

Minimalism Removes Petty Excuses.

At times, there are simply bustling seasons. Relatives might be in need; a chain of disastrous occasions may unfurl; we may get ourselves financially, emotionally, relationally or professionally overpowered.

But eventually, minimalism evacuates the negligible reasons why we can't accomplish those objectives we guarantee to have. Decluttering implies we never again have that "garage to clean" on a Saturday, and we can actually make it to our friend's child's birthday. Making more edge in our timetables implies we can't always say "I would, but I'm too busy."With excuses gone, we can concentrate on those practices that assistance us be our best selves.

Minimalism EncouragesIntentional Consumption.

People who are minimalists still create purchases– they simply make them even moreattentively, less rashly. At times, this implies spending practically nothing; different occasions this implies spending more to make purchase that have a positive (as opposed to negative) affect.

While the supply chain for huge numbers of our purchases is yet dark, we are ending up progressively mindful of the impact our purchases have on the world. For instance, fast fashion has been outed for its abusive (some of the time life compromising) influenceswomen and children in helplesscommunities.Minimalism allows us to be increasingly keen and compassionate in the manner in which we purchase necessities– from **food** and attires to toiletries and tools.

Minimalism Frees Up Time And Money.

People usually start to consider minimalist living when they conclude that they have more than they need, and that abundance is interfering with the life they want to live. Thus, the initial step usually includes disposing of stuff, and submitting not to purchase progressively extrain the future.

The naturaleffect is that money (that used to be spent on pointlessitems), as well as time (that used to be spent arranging or obtaining superfluous things), is currentlyfreed. The additional time and money on hand permits us to give more away; while minimalism will not really make us liberal, it will give us a superior reason to be.

Step by step instructions to begin: begin monitoring where your money is going – write it all. Toward the week's end, audit your list to perceive what was vital and what was not. Cut out those non-necessities!

Minimalism Is A Strong "No" For An Even Stronger "Yes".
There comes a moment that each minimalist gets herself alone with her needs. When we've said no to excessgoods and abundance activities, we get ourselves alone with our thoughts. What, then? We are compelled to choose what (or its identity) known to humankind that deserves our "yes".

I consider this is the moment that some world changer has to come to. This pivotal choice to express yes to that thing– that one thing we feel propelled to seek after, that trumps all else– is vital to having the effect we would like to make. Minimalism takes us to that moment, but bravery and belief (and community) enable us to step onward. When we havepermitted ourselves to oust the additional, we can say a wholehearted "yes" without thinking back.

I consider minimalism also draws out the best in humankind. It just takes a look at crazy Black Friday film to see that Western culture's cutting edge consumerist standardsare just playing wrong. Who cares if you have a 50-inch TV rather than a 30-inch set? Is it really worth prying things out of someone else's hands to make sure you can make a sparing? People were notborn to expend and end up caught in a cycle of purchasing stuff with expectations of hoisting their social status or filling an emotional gap.

ALEXANDRA JESSEN

HOW CAN MINIMALISM CHANGE SOCIETY?

Minimalism in Society

There is extraordinary power in the asking of these questions to actuallyredefine society.

At last, society and culture are what we as individual members make it. If every individual from our public asked these inquiries looking for more joyful lives, we would live in a different world. No doubt, this world would be significantly quieter, greater communityoriented, less harming to the environment, and, in particular, more joyful.

The proof for minimalism's things are clear: Every non-minimalist will start scrutinizing their assets, life activities, use of personal time, the experiences they want to make, and ability to contribute something useful. In actuality, minimalism has planted the seeds of progress. I realize it has influenced my life along these lines.

Even ifstrict minimalism does not spread that far, its message can resound with everybody, and I do mean everybody. It is an emphasis on living: Imagine a public strongly focused on the experiences that really matter.

MINIMALISM AND DECLUTTERING

The Power of Minimalism

Above all else, minimalism is a change in perspective. Its most prominent impact is urging individuals to think, see, and act toward another path: towards not so much realism, but rather more positive life experiences. Minimalism reclassifies the idea of life, regular and overall. Society trains us to join our status and notoriety to the things we possess – luxury brands, the most recent devices, or the most fashionable clothing. Minimalism instructs us to move far from this attitude.

The minimalist, like a researcher, asks,

› What does it mean to live?
› What are the fundamentals of an important life?
› Is that all we need to be cheerful?

It isan adventure looking for the fundamentals of living a cheerful and significant life. By removing clutter, concentrating on time and life experiences, the minimalist has couple of silly diversions to draw her into overconsumption and debt. It is an examination, one might say, to perceive what sort of lifestyle can realize the most bliss and importance. The ideal approach to begin, as all great science does, is with the fundamentals.

ALEXANDRA JESSEN

WAYS TO LIVE A HEALTHIER LIFESTYLE

Here are the absolute most significant ways minimalism has enhanced my life—and can enhance yours as well:

IDecluttered

The initial move toward a minimalist lifestyle is decluttering. What number of lipsticks and scents did I have? What number of CDs I never listened to? Pens, nail shines, shoes, outfits, designs… you get the image. My work area was cluttered with paper, note pads and office materials.

Having too much stuff has gotten under my skin. If you analyze how much moneyI'veexpended on all of it, you'll get a sum that will take your breath away. I would preferably not do that.

During the second day after I settled on the choice, I began the long, exhausting procedure of decluttering. I discarded the stuff and I was not even sad about the money I had spent on it. The time had come to settle on this drastic choice, so I could continue with a fresh start.

MINIMALISM AND DECLUTTERING

I saw that as I decluttered my environment, my psyche moved toward becoming clearer, too. I looked into a bit and found that other people felt a similar way. Minimalism can make you feel calmer.

Understand that minimalism is not just about materialism

Most people think minimalism implies disposing of stuff. While that is a decent initial step and the observable step, minimalism actually has to do with the advantages we experience once we are on the opposite side of de-cluttering, says Joshua Fields Millburn of The Minimalists. Those advantages, he says, extend to numerous unforeseen areas of life, from health and funds to relations and emotions. Millburn's books, narrative film, and podcast, all created with accomplice Ryan Nicodemus, incorporate heaps of tips identified with those different areas. But, he says, they all attach back to this underlying philosophy: "Minimalism is the thing that gets us past the things, so we can make room for life's most significant things, which really aren't things at all."

I have moreintentionality in my life.

Minimalism, above everything else, gets more intentionalitythat is prominent our lives. At first, we became intentional in the possessions we owned and brought into our home. But we before long found the introduce of "advance the most vital by evacuating each diversion" held promise and opportunity in innumerable aspects of life.

Figure out your finances with a "Need-Want-Like List"

Before minimalism, Millburn had a six-figure compensation, a major house, luxurycars, and costly clothes—as well as six-figure debt. Moneywasn't inherently awful," he says. "The issue was the choices I was making with the assets I had. So for me, minimalism was an approach to recapture control of how I use those assets. Millburn discovered a system that could work for other people. Wanting to understand where his money was going, he sat down and recorded eachcost from his home loan to his morning espresso. He then put all those costs into three classifications: Needs (necessities like sanctuary and nourishment), Wants (things you appreciate that increase the value of your life), and Likes (hasty purchases, like another new match of shoes). Then I took activity. In the firstmonth, I disposed of 100 percent of my Likes, which was not as difficult as it appeared. In the second month, I disposed of 100 percent of my Wants. The third month I decreased my Needs by moving to a smaller place and attempting other cost-sparing measures like utilizing less power, which spared me another 50 percent for each month. Once Millburn prevailing about escaping debt, he allowed himself to re-join the Wants that implied the most to him over into his life. "I got undeniably more incentive from those things because I knew if I was including something back in, I was doing as such with goal.

I have additional time and money than ever before.

Life is comprised of limited assets—money, time, energy, space (just to give some examples). By diminishing the quantity of physical belongings we claimed and purchased, we discovered a large number of those limited assets more accessible than any time in recent memory.

Reevaluate your relations

Millburn's minimalist way to deal with connections may at first stable brutal, but he urges individuals to listen to him: "Nearly all that I bring into my life, regardless of whether it's an ownership or a relationship, I must have the capacity to leave immediately." Many individuals remain involved with companions, spouses, and colleagues out of a feeling of carelessness or dread of progress, he clarifies. But an eagerness to leave what's commonplace methods you just hold the relations that genuinely convey an incentive to your life. "It sounds like a mystery, but my eagerness to leave has fortified the bonds I have with the nearest individuals in my life because we're not tied by commitment. If we're seeing someone's because we want to be, and we make the best within recent memory together." He adds a sort of aphorism to help keep relations in context (however, it pauses for a moment to soak in): "You can't change the people around you, but you can change the people around you.

I contrast myself less and other people.

We waste so much time and energy contrasting our lives with others. There is not a single euphoria in sight there. Investing all of our energy considering what we don't claim, causes us to miss valuing the things we do possess. Examination makes us feel we are passing up something—despite the fact that there is euphoria directly before us. Since discovering minimalism and craving less as opposed to additional, I contrast myself less and other individuals—in any event regarding physical belongings.

Feel Liberated

You think you have the things you purchase. You areoff base. When you have too a significant number of them,they have you. When you begin purchasing less stuff, you will feel free. This was one of the best exercises I learned since I settled on the choice.

I propose you complete a basic mental exercise today. After you declutter your space, sit in the live with your back straight and your eyes shut. Relax! Quiet yourself down. Envision how more straightforward your life will be when you have less stuff. Express this to yourself: "I don't need numerous things.

MINIMALISM AND DECLUTTERING

Starting now and into the foreseeable future, I'll be getting just the things I need." Repeat this activity each and every day.

It took just a couple of days of this rehearsing this activity and I saw I never again was taking a gander at garments and different things to purchase on the web. It's like you're sending that message to your subliminal dimensions, and that is where the longing originates from.

I measure the estimation of work in all the more satisfying terms.

Work gets talked about in too numerous undesirable terms—both inside and outside minimalist circles. Inside minimalist circles, work can frequently be viewed as something to be stayed away from. I take a different perspective. Work is satisfying when found in the correct setting.

I have found shrouded gifts and passions.

Minimalism, I assume, does not change our abilities or aptitudes. But it opens up chance to seek after them in manners we hadn't envisioned previously. All the while, it might uncover shrouded gifts and passions we never knew existed. Composing, is the best precedent in my life.

When we beat the compulsion to waste our most limited assets basically overseeing and seeking after an ever increasing number of physical belongings, it's stunning what else we find we can do well. This fills much more passion for living (as I referenced previously).

Remain careful

Minimalists live intentionally. If there is something in your life that you don't love, change it! When I began my minimalist adventure, I was in an occupation and a relationship that didn't serve me. Inside a half year, I was out of both of those, and more joyful than I'd at any point been. I like to consider what my optimal life resembles, and then work toward that. Removing the things that aren't serving you are the initial step to making the life that you want. An activity that really encourages me is to record what a perfect day would look like for you in five years time. At that point move in the direction of that objective.

Found MyWeaknesses

Minimalism implies being focused on the most basic needs. I began eating straightforward nourishment, wearing basic garments and settling on basic choices. It wasn't that easy. My mind played nasty traps on me.

For what reason don't I purchase only one more paper on the web? I'll begin chipping away at my own articles next time.

This dress is so adorable. It's on markdown. I'll never get this cost when I need it.

MINIMALISM AND DECLUTTERING

When I began persuading myself to get something I didn't totally need, I was finding my shortcomings. For what reason am I so connected to these things I want to purchase? It is safe to say that they are really improving my life? If the appropriate response is no, then I don't get them!

I have left a case for my children they will always remember.
Throughout the previous ten years, I have displayed for my kids that individual effects are not the way to joy, that security is found in their character, and the quest for bliss runs a different street than most promotions will let you know. These are important life exercises I expectation will shape their choices far into what's to come.

Wound up Conscious about the Way I Spend Money
Planning is certifiably not a fun activity. All things considered, it's something we totally need to do when endeavoring to set aside somemoney and carry on with a minimalist life. When I'm focused on spending less, I know where my money is going.

Here's my recommendation to you: Try monitoring your vital costs. Make needs. Pay the bills first. Then, get the nourishment you need for the week. Keep things insignificant! Try not to get nourishment you will discard.

ALEXANDRA JESSEN

You'll understand you're sparing a great deal of money directly after you begin rehearsing this strategy. You'll monitor all your costs, so you'll know when some of them are a bit much.

I have developed in my confidence and otherworldliness.

I don't compose much about my own confidence and spirituality—it's simply not something I do (however it's not elusive if you're searching for it). But as I think back more than ten years of minimalism, I can't disregard the effect and impact that minimalism has had on my spirituality—not that it has transformed my trust, but rather it has surely conveyed new profundity to it. And for that, I am eternally thankful.

Outside minimalist circles, work is that thing you do to profit as conceivable to purchase as much stuff as conceivable. This too, is unfortunate and narrow minded. Work is our main thing to convey advantage to society and the general population around us. When we do our function admirably, everybody benefits. Minimalism has caused me to see work in another, additionally satisfying light.

I took back control of my own life.

While I didn't have any acquaintance with it at the time, my choice to claim less was eventually about reclaiming control. It was tied in with reclaiming a control I didn't understand I had surrendered. It was tied in with saying no

MINIMALISM AND DECLUTTERING

to societal weight and social standards and settling on the choice to live individually terms. Minimalism gives that advantage to all who seek after it.

I have more passion for living.

A satisfied life is a passionate life. A life spent seeking after things that issue inhales energy and force into our days. It isn't difficult to get up toward the beginning of the day when you realize your days mean an option that is more prominent than yourself. Minimalism diverted my life's energy toward quest for more prominent significance than material belongings—and impelled more passion because of it.

It's Easy to Pair Outfits

What amount of time do you think Mark Zuckerberg spends attempting to make sense of what to wear? My estimate isno time. He spares his energy and time for progressively essential things. He presumably wears whatever he sees first in the storage room.

That is the excellence of a minimalistic lifestyle. I pick random things and they go superbly well together. I picked them in view of straightforwardness, so all hues and plans are correlative.

I have achieved things I never envisioned conceivable.

ALEXANDRA JESSEN

Ten years prior, I never would have envisioned my life would look today like it actually does. This blog is perused by 1 million different people each and every month. I've composed books—with another one turning out soon. I began a magazine and established a charitable association changing vagrant consideration around the globe. I've talked all over the world. And I've been met for papers and radio shows and podcasts. All the more imperatively, I have been increasingly occupied with my children's lives and marriage than at any other time.

THE KEY ASPECTS TO MINIMALISM

While a minimalistic life will appear to be unique from one individual to the next, there are sure core values you should use to begin. You should concentrate on three things: expelling needless things, sustaining the basics, and making the most of your activities.

Evacuating needless things

As referenced above, evacuating needless things doesn't equivalent to precluding everything or discarding your assets. The attention is on the word 'needless' and the definition you apply to this word. You need to identify the things and activities in your life, which you need and value.

In minimalism, you want to impartially take a gander at every thing and think about its actual importance and incentive to you. To some it may mean expelling assets, for example, extravagant furnishings or scaling back to a smaller condo, while others may concentrate on decreasing their closet or shoe gathering.

Identifying needless things probably won't be as easy as it sounds. We will in general place a great deal of wistful incentive to things, as well as consider thefuture conceivable outcomes. For instance, it's easy to take a gander at your bread creator and persuade yourself you may need it later on. The key is to identify the reasons you value the specific thing and understand whether youactuallyneed it.

Notice that having less doesn't mean you can't have things or even add new things to your life. It's just about identifying the things you actually require and which add to your overall satisfaction.

Supporting the basics
Minimalism's basic standards also incorporate supporting the fundamentals. These naturally incorporate life's necessities, for example, nourishment, water and safe house. But you'll also have different fundamentals essential to yourself.

By making a note of the things that have the greatest effect on your bliss and prosperity, you can begin sustaining these aspects of your life more. You'll in all probability also identify the needless aspects of your assets and activities.

Make sure to take a gander at the above inquiries through both your private and work life. Minimalism isn't just about carrying on with a minimalistic lifestyle at home in your private

MINIMALISM AND DECLUTTERING

space, but also about identifying the fundamentals in your vocation.

Making the most of your activities

The last rule manages making the most of your activities. You want to begin evading things that don't make a difference to you or add to your prosperity and satisfaction.

Each move you make and each purchase you make ought to have a significance behind it. These activities ought to positively affect your life.

Making the most of your activities is to a great extent about supportability as well. It's not just about the momentary effect or joy, but the long haul affect.

Another vehicle may satisfy you for multi month, but following a year, you may be tired of seeing it.

Rather than searching for the transient reward and effect, you want to discover the things and activities that keep on having an impact long into what's to come.

ALEXANDRA JESSEN

PRACTICAL WAYS TO SIMPLIFY YOUR LIFE

Decide Your Vision

As with anything new you acquaint into your life pointed with change or better it, you need to realize what you're attempting to accomplish.

This could be characterized as finding your why.

The vision may be as basic as decluttering your home and pressing lighter when voyaging or as comprehensive as a shifting your whole lifestyle or scaling back your habitation. The fact of the matter is you have a dream at the top of the priority list and base your choices around it.

Asking yourself the why, what, how, when and who can help steer you the correct way.

> › Why would you like to bring components of minimalism into your life?
> › What benefits would you say you are endeavoring to get?
> › How does the perfect state look when you picture it?
> › When would you like to begin and to what extent will it take to achieve that state?

MINIMALISM AND DECLUTTERING

> › Who else will be a piece of this procedure and shift?

For me, the vision is only simplification by decreasing clutter (physically and mentally) so as to save my time and energy to concentrate more on what conveys an incentive to my life.

Work On Being Paper Free

To proceed with the computerized cleaning topic above, getting to be sans paper as most ideal is an open door given on account of the advanced world.

Regardless of whether it's magazines, papers, books, charges, reports for work or other mail and paper products, it's truly easy to fill space around the home and office.

Nonetheless, the vast majority of those have a computerized answer for help limit the physical clutter.

> › Kindle (or other tablet) to house your books and magazines
> › Turning all bills, articulations and key correspondence to email over paper mail
> › Schedule paper cleanses, like our minimalism review, to help keep it a need
> › Digitize your archives with photographs on your telephone or tablet and then spare them digitally
> › Encourage collaborators to print less records and be a pioneer in that space
> › Rethink how much paper towel, napkins and bathroom tissue you're utilizing

The hardest piece of this paper free attitude for me is certainly the books.

I've constantly cherished adding new books to the rack. Regardless of whether it's the discussions they can begin, the chance to loan to other people or only an inborn accumulating attitude, this will be the hardest of the minimalism tips for me to completely actualize.

Complete A Minimalism Audit

So as to begin the change and shift your lifestyle, it's useful to realize what you're managing in general.

Enter the minimalism review.

This could incorporate a review of possibly either of the physical merchandise and the psychological side of what's creation your life progressively mind boggling or muddled. The key is it's associated with your vision above and what YOU want.

Potential areas to consider with your review:

> Home
> Office
> Car
> Subscriptions and Services
> Digital Activity
> Habits
> Thoughts
> Tasks

MINIMALISM AND DECLUTTERING

Basically, if you're hoping to simplify your life you need to think about all aspects of it. Review your present circumstance to best understand the open doors accessible to achieve your objectives.

Another strategy to help reviewing your life is to play out a period track of all that you do from the minute you wake up until the point that you hit the hay.

Toggl is an administration that encourages you do only that with their straightforward (yet ground-breaking) time following application. Toggl gives you a comprehensive understanding of where your time is being gone through with their detailing highlights. It's a paid stage but they offer a free multi day preliminary.

Begin Small
In indistinguishable vein from another eating routine or wellness schedule, it's generally best practice to begin moderate with your minimalism outlook.

Making a plunge head initially can be compelling and fast-track the achievement you're attempting to accomplish. Be that as it may, it can also prompt errors or getting wore out.

The last thing you want to do is move all that you claim or change too much and understand this wasn't the lifestyle you wanted.

› Pick one propensity to actualize that underpins your vision
› Fill one tote sack of garments to give
› Alter a couple of components of your day by day schedule
› Start with one room in your house

Small successes, make energy.

Pick one spotlight territory previously based on your vision and starting review. Begin small and master that before moving onto the following need or opportunity.

Swing Clutter To Money

As far as the physical side of minimalism, a frequently ignored profit by actualizing some minimalism into your life is turning your clutter to money.

When I chose to put taking control of my money and life as a best need, one of the primary easy money related successes I had immediately was moving $1,800 worth of "stuff".

These were things that aggregated in my capacity unit, in the storage room, under the bed, on the rack, and so on over forever and a day of amassing. They were once in a while, if regularly, being used or giving any an incentive to my life.

A large portion of the people I converse with have had a comparative experience or store of "stuff" developed.

MINIMALISM AND DECLUTTERING

Regardless of whether it's a one-time scrub to begin simplifying your life that at that point turns into a yearly review, turn that clutter to money and use those assets towards your money related objectives.

Decluttr

Decluttr is a free application and site that allows you to turn the "stuff" you've collected into money. It's strength is electronic, tech things, computer games, DVDs, and so forth and even lego.

You just output the scanner tag (ISBN) of the thing with the Decluttr application and Decluttr gives you a quick offer. They then send you a prepaid delivery name and settle your installments after they've gotten your things. No closeouts, no expenses and an easy to use application (or web) stage. Additionally you can get to free sending and protection inclusion on your things.

Be Honest and Embrace It

A standout amongst the best minimalism tips I've taken from different web journals, podcasts and content regarding the matter is to be straightforward.

Especially when you're simply beginning to endeavor to simplify your life.

This applies at as high of a dimension as your overall vision with minimalism and down to the granular dimension of "do I really need this coat?".

Regardless of whether you simply want a cleaner, progressively sorted out front room or to scale back your SUV, genuineness will assume a key job.

Given the potential changes coming could be a drastic shift, you will want to grasp it. What preferable approach to do that over gain from others and associate with other seeking after a minimalist, more straightforward lifestyle.

There are a huge number of individuals web based looking to declutter, simplify, expel pressure and carry on with a progressively healthy lifestyle.

Be straightforward, grasp it and associate.

Play out A Digital Cleaning
Decluttering doesn't need to just incorporate the physical materials you forces. The computerized world we as a whole regular so frequently gives various basic approaches to bring minimalism into your life too.

What areas of your online propensities and cell phone utilization actually convey value? Which are additional time and mind wasters than helpful? Would you be able to simplify the advanced world's job in your life?

Some prevalent arrangements depending your circumstance may include:

› Reduce email memberships
› Limit program tabs open

MINIMALISM AND DECLUTTERING

> Keep a negligible number of bookmarks
> Set a specific time for browsing email
> Disconnect from gadgets at select occasions
> Delete pointless applications from your telephone

Contingent upon your profession, family and living circumstance certain things won't be feasible You need to discover what works and advantages you.

Keep in mind It's More Than Just Physical Items

The principal thing that frequently strikes a chord for some (counting myself) when you consider minimalism is likely a cutting edge flat with constrained furnishings. Most likely white walls, two seats, small table, one encircled picture and a plant.

That is clearly a speculation.

It's a mentality, change in lifestyle, shift in propensities, new viewpoint and a great deal more. There can be ecological, financial, social and emotional wellness benefits.

It tends to be anything YOU desire it to be.

Separating of superfluous physical things to decrease clutter is obviously part of the condition but it's something other than that.

Value Experiences Over Materials

A typical amateur minimalism tip is to value experiences over materials. Use the assets you have, regardless of whether it's time or money, to appreciate "living" over gathering.

In the realm of simplifying your life, valueing experiences over materials can have various advantages – for your psyche, wallet, lifestyle, health and more.

Manufacture new abilities by taking courses and classes.

Sort out experiences for you, your family, companions and friends and family.

Possibly it's a parity of experiences and things. Possibly it's vigorously tilted to experiences. You need to ask yourself what conveys more an incentive to your life.

STEPS TO A MINIMALIST LIFESTYLE

When you've met the choice to carry on with an increasingly oversimplified life, you'll be defied with the inquiry how you will approach this gigantic task. You want to simplify your life, but the multifaceted nature of the task is terrifying. There are such a large number of things that aggregated during the time that you don't realize where in any case. In the meantime, such a significant number of difficult inquiries need to be tended to. Limiting essentially can feel in these circumstances too enormous of a challenge. The sheer size of the minimalism challenge can be very overpowering, especially before all else.

But stress not. You don't need to minimalize your whole life from one day to the next. While there are extraordinary cases of people who dispose of all that they have starting with one day then onto the next, this may not really be the best alternative for you. When it comes to minimalism, it's critical to just simply begin. It's not all that imperative to achieve the goal (for example a minimalist lifestyle) promptly. Rather, minimalism is a voyage. Make small strides and begin completing one thing after another. Dispose of one superfluous belonging at any given moment. Kill one diverting movement after another. Along these lines you will make the progress to a minimalist life much smoother.

The basic thought and procedure of minimalism can be abridged in two stages. The initial step comprises of identifying what is vital and significant to you. The second step comprises of disposing of basically everything that isn't fundamental and does not increase the value of your life. As easy as this sounds, this can be a significant complex process. Consequently, it's useful to part the whole procedure of limiting your life into easier advances that can be tended to in a steady progression.

Here are the fundamental advances you can take to simplify your life and to live more minimalistic.

Assess your life.

Set needs. At the foundation of turning into a minimalist lies an examination of your life. It's the first and maybe most essential advance towards simplifying your life. Indeed, this progression is important to the point that it must not be ignored. What you want to do During this assessment of your life is to identify what's most significant and essential to you. Discover what components of your life include the bestvalue, satisfaction and importance to

MINIMALISM AND DECLUTTERING

your life. Doing as such will assist you with settingyour needs straight. With an unmistakable understanding of what's really imperative to you, it's a lot easier to start the way toward limiting. Organizing encourages you to understand the advantages of making room in your life for the fundamental. Without this sort of understanding, you probably won't feel all too OK with disposing of insignificant things you've become used to. For example, if you try to quit staring at the TV, you may have a difficult time when you don't know absolutely for what reason you're doing it for. Be that as it may, if you understand that you surrender TV to have more opportunity to go through with a movement that really satisfies you, you'll be bound to oversee things. You can begin assessing your life by making a short rundown. Record the most essential things in your life and focus on these first. Concentrate on gradually making more space in your life for your needs.

Declutter

Regardless of whether you see it or not, clutter has a tremendous impact on your life. If you're in the propensity for shopping on the web when you feel exhausted or worried, you likely have heaps of clutter — things you may not focus on, garments you never wear, books you'll never peruse and contraptions you never again use. You don't need to consume all your common belongings to be a minimalist, but you should make a move if you have heaps of clutter in your home, office or elsewhere in your life.

Begin small. Consume it space by room, storeroom by wardrobe and cabinet by cabinet, until the point that you can sift through your effects and choose what needs to remain and what can go. You will feel a load lifting off your shoulders as your breathing room expands. Physical clutter will just divert you, so center your time and energy around controlling this aspect of your life. It will no uncertainty require investment to get yourself into the best possible attitude where you automatically stop and think before you purchase things. But up to that point, this is a begin.

Another approach to keep your life decluttered is to live in a smaller space. Small homes have picked up in prominence of late as an option in contrast to bigger flats, apartment suites or homes with superfluous space. If you have a smaller living space, you won't have space to store things you needn't bother with. Decreasing the measure of your living space can also be unfathomably financially savvy, as well as more eco-accommodating. While there are numerous advantages to owning a little home, making it easier to carrying on with a minimalist lifestyle is one of the best ones.

MINIMALISM AND DECLUTTERING

Choose One Clutter-Free Zone

Endeavoring to declutter your house is most likely too much. I unquestionably wouldn't prescribe doing it the manner in which I did!

Rather, name one space to be your without clutter zone. That could be your room, your lounge room, your carport – any room you feel could profit by de-cluttering the most.

Put aside an end of the week to really concentrate on making this room your aggregate sans clutter zone – look at my advisers for decluttering here for a few tips and exhortation! Having one room gotten out is also an incredible method to test whether you really want to wind up a minimalist and what amount having a without clutter space benefits you.

Do some exploration.

If you're perusing this at that point you're on the initial step to carrying on with a magnificent minimalist life. While many individuals may have found out about it, there are a great deal of confusions associated with minimalism. It is therefore reasonable to initially understand what the lifestyle is all about.

Sites, for example, theminimalist.com offer great rules into how to leave the lifestyle and notwithstanding refering to other people who are carrying on with the lifestyle. At the end of the day, learn as much as you can about the lifestyle and guarantee you are clear of all the misinterpretations.

Assess your assets.

After you've set your needs, it's an ideal opportunity to address your material belongings. Consider all that you claim and see whether these things line up with your needs. Investigate every possibility and question everything. Make sense of if the things you possess increase the value of your life or if they just occupy you and make mental commotion. It's regularly difficult to concede, but the assessment of your assets may feature that you possess very numerous things of next to zero value. These assets might be extravagant or engaging "pleasant to-have's," but where it counts ourselves we realize that they don't include any significant importance or reason to our lives. All they do is waste our time, deplete our energy or void our financial balances. Accumulate a rundown with all your assets that are repetitive and no longer of significant worth to you. Begin moderate by disposing of a couple of these things every week.

Unplug Once in a While

Try not to be reluctant to unplug yourself from your gadgets now and then so you can concentrate on different things occurring in the present. Truly, online networking can be addictive and come as a second nature, but it's essential to eliminate your use. It's also

MINIMALISM AND DECLUTTERING

undesirable to always come close yourself to other people, which is our main thing, regardless of whether we like to let it be known or not.

Studies demonstrate a few people check their gadgets each 6.5 minutes. Try not to be that individual. Enhance your in-person associations with individuals for an all the more compensating experience.

Relish the here and now — what's going on in your life minute by minute. If you're continually seeing the world through your telephone screen or by concentrating on what you don't have or aren't doing, it's a lot harder to gain experiences and investigate new things. Consider it. If you go to a show and take pictures and recordings the whole time, you'll miss a great deal of aspects of the experience. Be available, be careful and live at the time.

Keep in mind, toning it down would be ideal. You don't need to surrender all the material things you appreciate — you simply want to have a sheltered harmony between those things and what is realistically vital in your life. Concentrate less on your assets, and more on your overall joy.

Assess how you invest your energy.
Turning into a minimalist isn't just about de-cluttering physical items, but also about disposing of time-wasting exercises. The third

step is therefore all about making sense of how you invest vast parts of your energy. Ask yourself the inquiry if the exercises you participate in increase the value of your life. Doing as such will assist you with spending less time with inefficient or even time-wasting exercises. This thusly will give you the opportunity of possessing more energy for the exercises you really appreciate. Take a gander at all that you do and each movement you consistently take part in. Record how much time you go through with pretty much purposeless exercises. See whether there are exercises that include positively no value. Identify if your responsibilities are in accordance with your needs. When you have a decent understanding on how you invest your energy, check whether you can decrease unbeneficial exercises. Begin moderate by tending to the most problems that need to be addressed, each one in turn. It's smarter to free your life for the last time of one negative action than attempting to battle a few ones indifferently.

Diminish the bang.

When you've checked what you have, you would then be able to get to the useless stuff and dispose of it. Minimalism is basically about living with what you just need. For instance, you really needn't bother with a vehicle if open transportcould fill in as an adequate elective methods. Taking out the pointless things from your life decreases both the waste and the psychological exertion that sorting out those things go up against you.

Assess who you invest your energy with.

The general population you invest the vast majority of your energy with have an extraordinary impact upon your life. It's therefore just coherent that you want to support associations with constructive and empowering individuals. In the meantime, minimalism is tied in with identifying people who are nothing else except for lethal. Identify the people who deplete your energy and waste your time. Begin by investing less energy with the individuals who do only drag you down and demoralize you from seeking after your fantasies.

Set points of confinement.

When turning into a minimalist, you will find that there are sure exercises/things you just can't or don't want to dispose of. We as a whole have exercises we do frequently and can't manage without. You may need your telephone to make essential business calls. You may need your PC and web access to compose messages and to remain educated. So also, you may at present be keen on perusing rousing RSS channels or tuning in to motivating podcasts. The way to all these exercises is to set proper points of confinement. Try not to give these exercises a chance to meddle with your life. Try not to give them a chance to interfere with your work process. Rather, center around participating in these exercises just amid specified occasions. Set clear points of confinement to the recurrence you browse your messages – twice day by day is all that anyone could need. Set points of confinement for all that you routinely take part in. It will assist you with being increasingly gainful and focused.

Dispose Of Stuff And Be Clutter Free

The decluttering procedure is the easiest method to kick begin your adventure to minimalism. Doing this gradually and in a couple of scopes is by all accounts the most productive. I did around three or four ranges of decluttering before I was totally happy with all that I disposed of, and all that I kept. When you experience the decluttering procedure at a reasonable pace (for instance, don't do it all in one day or even in multi month), the change will be somewhat easier.

If you go from a full house to a for the most part void house medium-term, it will be an a lot harder change. It functioned admirably for me to attempt to hit around 5 areas for every week – and I picked small areas, like one work area cabinet or simply the sweaters in my storage room. Numerous individuals like to declutter by the room, so if that works for you begin there.

MINIMALISM AND DECLUTTERING

In spite of the fact that it takes more time to declutter gradually, it is a lot easier to keep up a minimalist lifestyle if the decluttering procedure is done gradually and cautiously.

Choose what's critical.
You need to identify just things with genuine incentive to you. A ton of garbage that we keep can be credited to 'simply in case I need this' but I very uncertainty that you will need that vacant ramen bowl you've been importance to work into a DIY foot stool installation for the past 8 months. If you can't locate a fair use for a thing, dispose of it.

Dispose of the abundance.
Over disposing of the pointless, one ought to also dispose of the overabundance. For example, you don't really need numerous pots and skillet nor do your pets need such a significant number of beds. Abundance just uses up space that you could commit to something increasingly critical or leave unfilled. There is no need to fill each alcove and corner with a thing from your movements or some other kind of things that just serves to draw the eye. The objective ought to be to have all your assets fill a need and be utilitarian.

Get objectives.
Minimalism is predominantly a tool to accomplish a more joyful lifestyle. Therefore, to start carrying on with a minimalist lifestyle, it implies you should have an objective. This can be anything from decreasing heading out or

over the top spending to better your vocation or meet your own objectives.

Lift Productivity With Minimalist Work Habits

We invest a great deal of energy at work, so it's critical to have a minimalist home as well as a minimalist office. Taking command over all aspects of your life will prompt less pressure, better time the executives, increased pay, and a superior work life balance.

The greatest increases in my pay and satisfaction with my work all originated from being purposeful in my life. When I settled on the life I wanted I was ready to leave my old corporate activity and begin my very own business, profiting that I at any point longed for. Building great propensities is a lot easier as a minimalist because we complete one critical thing that the vast majority don't do: we took an opportunity to understand what's vital to use and rolled out purposeful improvements to carry on with a superior life. That puts us route in front of the vast majority and the prizes are found in our own lives and in our profession.

Quit rationalizing.

A minimalist lifestyle has drawbacks. It requires enough self-control and genuineness to dissect things that offer no an incentive past a simply tasteful one. Extravagances and different overabundances are to be stayed away from if they don't help fill a need. This can turn out to be a challenge especially for an individual who is brimming with excuses.

Shop just for basics.

Minimalism doesn't mean you quit looking for products and enterprises. It keeps up on looking for basics. This is so as to guarantee that they don't waste assets on the pointless. The aftereffect of this is the general population wind up focusing their endeavors just on vital undertakings adapted towards them accomplishing their objectives.

Simplify Your Diet For Simple Meals

A straightforward eating regimen doesn't mean a bland eating routine or having a similar thing again and again. I initially begun by understanding my kitchen clutter and making sense of what I really need in my kitchen. When I thinned down the key fundamentals I discovered I delighted in cooking more, I currently anticipate getting back home and planning new dishes for all my suppers. Having an all around supplied, but simplified wash room helped a great deal towards this.

Like everything with minimalism, it's critical to make sense of what is ideal for you and streamline things keeping that in mind. A few people have an amazingly basic eating regimen of rice and beans, others discover a plant based eating routine or minimalist crude vegetarian diet to be appropriate for them. For me I begin with my most loved dishes and deciding a base arrangement of fixings that I generally keep on hand.

Quit storing.

Gathering pointless things eats into the space saved for things that could more readily serve the person. To battle this, it is essential to keep away from the gathering of pointless things. Also, give things that are not needed to the individuals who might be ideally serviced by them.

Make arrangements.

The most ideal approach to accomplish objectives is to guarantee that there are plans set up for accomplishing the objectives. Plans are especially critical to new minimalists as they have more reality with the appropriation of this new lifestyle. Making arrangements puts the person in the best position to accomplish his objectives and make use of the assets that minimalism gives.

Travel delicately.

Each time you take an adventure, simply convey a couple of things to limit stuff and wastage. Voyaging delicately guarantees you just move around with fundamental things and nothing more. For example, you can pack just a large portion of the garments you need.

Grasp multipurpose tools.

Rather than utilizing numerous tools that all fill different needs, why not have a solitary tool that fills a huge number of needs. This is the advantage that minimalists are urged to search for in all their things. Multipurpose tools ration the space that could have been used up by having numerous tools to accomplish a similar objective. Why by a screw driver and a corkscrew while the Swiss Army Knife accompanies the two tools in a smaller plan.

Simplify Your Diet For Simple Meals

A basic eating regimen doesn't mean a bland eating regimen or having a similar thing again and again. I originally begun by understanding my kitchen clutter and making sense of what I really need in my kitchen. When I thinned down the key basics I discovered I delighted in cooking more, I currently anticipate getting back home and planning crisp dishes for all my suppers. Having a very much loaded, but simplified wash room helped a ton towards this.

Like everything with minimalism, it's essential to make sense of what is ideal for you and streamline things keeping that in mind. A few people have an incredibly straightforward eating routine of rice and beans, others discover a plant based eating regimen or minimalist crude vegetarian diet to be appropriate for them. For me I begin with my most loved dishes and deciding a base arrangement of fixings that I generally keep on hand.

Less internet based life is an or more.

Diminishing clutter in a minimalist's life also implies decreasing the measure of time wasted in devouring non-accommodating data. While internet based life can be an amazing asset for correspondence and business, it generally fills in as a stage for people to share vain and generally non-supportive titbits about their lives that you as a minimalist will have no use for. Web based life also urges spending because of innumerable customer focused on Ads.

Digitize everything.

Books and papers can be lumbering and space devouring. Be that as it may, advanced configurations for information and data can sit in your multipurpose tool and allow you hold an a lot bigger clump when contrasted with real physical content. It helps if you begin getting as much computerized substance as you can. digital books, online papers, music downloads rather than CDs, all these assistance guarantee that you don't fill your own space with pointless clutter.

Obtain whatever you don't need to purchase.

While it might be decent to possess you claim things, minimalists are urged to rather get things that they would use as opposed to getting them. This decreases the quantity of assets they have and guarantees they don't pile on clutter or store things. As long as you keep the obtained things safe and the loan

MINIMALISM AND DECLUTTERING

specialist wouldn't fret sharing, like to acquire things as opposed to getting them.

Continuously pick quality over amount.

This is for the basic truth that quality things last longer than shabby options. Whenever you choose to purchase a thing, get one with the most elevated quality accessible. It will last you longer and guarantee that you do need to continue supplanting it and heaping up trash.

Financial plan your time.

Similarly as you spending plan your assets, spending plan your time. Guarantee that all the things you try to do are equipped towards edifying you. Try not to get things done for the only for it but appreciate whatever time you spend accomplishing something.

Representative as much as conceivable.

As frequently as conceivable, value your time and guarantee that all tasks that can be executed by another person are given to another person. This is in order to give the minimalist more opportunity to execute the tasks increasingly critical to them or those that the minimalist is better prepared to perform.

Before getting a thing, dispose of another.

One great principle guideline for the minimalist is to guarantee that before influencing a purchase of something, to dispose of any things officially claimed. This secures against clutter and the handling too numerous things.

Dispose of emotional clutter.
Similarly as the physical clutter can eat into physical space, emotional clutter can eat up mental space. In an offer to carry on with a minimalist lifestyle, evade emotional things and rather find sound outlets to guarantee your psychological state mirrors your physical space.

Separate an incentive from material things.
In turning into a decent minimalist, one needs to quit setting too much an incentive on material belongings. This is just feasible by setting significance on fundamental materials.

Eat straightforward and solid sustenances.
The minimalist lifestyle stretches out to dietary patterns. One ought to eat nourishments that meet sustenance standards and make an effort not to over enjoy pointlessly costly nourishments. The sustenances ought to also be basic enough to get ready.

Choose to carry on with a superior life.
The general purpose of minimalist living is to encourage more joyful, progressively fulfilled living. The minimalist needs to chip away at doing precisely this by grasping increasingly beautiful aspects of living and abstaining from

wasting time on getting a charge out of pleasures don't enhance personal satisfaction.

Make an investment account.

Monetary opportunity is a piece of minimalism. Having a bank account and frequently sending money to the record urges you to proceed notwithstanding carrying on with a progressively minimalist lifestyle because it will guarantee you cut out needless memberships and costs. Additionally, it will make you all the more financially steady.

Dress with less.

Having few shoes, garments and extras may sound extraordinary but it is a decent method to start carrying on with a minimalist lifestyle. It makes life less intricate and decreases clutter in your closet.

Appreciate the voyage of carrying on with a minimalist lifestyle.

Finally, when you've embraced or chosen to carry on with a minimalist lifestyle, welcome the seemingly insignificant details you have and in every case live each and every day expressing gratitude toward yourself for the way you've taken.

Quit multitasking.

There is no such thing as multitasking. It is a legend, a fantasy. Numerous individuals have faith in it and pride themselves of being astounding multitaskers. But all they do is to trick themselves. Firmly having faith in something does not really make it genuine. Scientific research has indicated on many occasions that the human cerebrum isn't fit for multitasking. All you do is to change starting with one movement then onto the next, which can drastically decrease your efficiency. Try not to clutter your work process and life by seeking after different exercises all the while. Rather, center around doing just a single thing at any given moment. Do whatever you do with the best consideration and consideration. Dispose of diversions and endeavor to conquer the compulsion to multitask. "Singletasking" will assist you with being increasingly gainful in what you do. It increases your focus and will dramatically affect the yield of your work. Minimalism is tied in with concentrating on what's really critical – with more prominent consideration.

Assess your objectives and desire.

We as a whole have objectives. They influence us to get up every morning to proceed with the quest for our fantasies. Our objectives and desire significantly shape the lives we are living. But not all objectives are advantageous. Not all desire are good with a minimalistic lifestyle. It is therefore essential to assess if your objectives are still in accordance with the needs you set in stage 1 of this list. Question if the quest for your objectives will increase the value of your life. Set aside yourself opportunity to ponder the result of your objectives. Is it the result deserving of

MINIMALISM AND DECLUTTERING

your time and exertion? In the meantime, it's critical to lessen the measure of objectives you seek after. Try not to clutter your life with a wide assortment of objectives that you seek after just pitifully. Concentrate on setting yourself a predetermined number of objectives and seek after these with your most prominent consideration and tirelessness. You could even venture to such an extreme as to minimalize to just a single objective. It will push you to enormously diminish pressure and to focus on the objective with the most noteworthy need.

Begin small.

When it comes to simplifying your life, it's critical to keep up a slow dimension of progress. If you set yourself the yearning objective to de-clutter your whole house or level inside about fourteen days, you may overpower yourself. Rather, begin small and work yourself gradually towards an increasingly shortsighted presence. Rather than cleansing a whole room, center around smaller areas of the room. Complete one region at once until the point that the whole room is not so much cluttered but rather more minimalistic. For example, center around de-cluttering one segment of your rack after another.

Live purposely.

Another imperative aspect of turning into a minimalist is to live right now and to live more intentionally. To do this current, it's imperative to shift your consideration from the past or future to this exact second. Do whatever it takes not to point the finger at yourself for what occurred in the past and attempt to quit agonizing over what's to come. When you live in the past or the future, you deny the present snapshot of its delight and power. Understand that you can neither make things that occurred in the past fixed nor would you be able to impact what occurs later on. Rather, use the present to construct the fundament for a more promising time to come. Correspondingly, use the experiences/botches you've made in the past as imperative exercises. Living all the more intentionally will assist you with spending your time in a progressively significant and important way. Simplify your life and investigate the satisfaction living at the time has to offer.

Limit screen time and media utilization.

The time we spend on mechanical devices adds pointless commotion to our lives. Also, the negligent utilization of media includes more intricacy than it simplifies. If you spend a lot of your tedious different types of media (TV, films, Internet, papers, and so forth.) at that point these things will significantly shape the manner in which you think and feel. The additional time you go through with media, the more impact it will apply over your life. If media utilization commands your life, your contemplations and activities will be ruled by it as well. It can extraordinarily influence your convictions and your general point of view. The huge issue, be that as it may, is to completely grasp the impact of media at the forefront of your thoughts. This is especially difficult if your reasoning is still extraordinarily impacted by media. There's solitary one approach to find the negative effect of all these things on your life, which is by subsequently disposing of them from your life. It's moderately easy to disregard the above as hogwash if you're still intensely impacted by media. But you will be astounded of the significant difference disengaging and turning things off can make.

Ask yourself

Does this assistance to live more minimalistic? You can incredibly contribute to the minimization of your life by settling on choices that are more in accordance with a minimalistic lifestyle. If you can do this, your purchasing propensities will incredibly change. This thusly will assist you with avoiding decluttering your life in any case. So whenever you will meet a choice, ask yourself if it will help you minimalize or if it just includes pointless clamor. Offer yourself the conversation starter if the choice you will meet will simplify your life or not. If it doesn't contribute to a minimalist lifestyle, rethink if it is the best alternative for you.

ALEXANDRA JESSEN

SIMPLE WAYS TO SAVE MONEY

Set a reserve funds objective

Use our Savings calculatorto perceive how your reserve funds will develop.

A few people think that its difficult to get persuaded about sparing, but it's frequently a lot easier if you set an objective.

Your initial step is to have some crisis reserve funds – money to fall back on if you have a crisis, for example, an evaporator breakdown or if you can't work for some time.

Attempt to get three months of costs in an easy or moment get to account.

Try not to stress if you can't spare this straight away, but keep it as an objective to go for.

The most ideal approach to set aside extra money is to pay some money into a bank account each month.

When you've put aside your secret stash, conceivable funds objectives to consider may include:

MINIMALISM AND DECLUTTERING

› Buying a vehicle without applying for a new line of credit
› Taking an occasion without stressing over the bills when you get back
› Having some additional money to draw on while you're on maternity or paternity leave

Record your costs

The initial step to setting aside some money is to make sense of the amount you spend. Monitor all your costs—that implies each espresso, household thing and money tip. When you have your information, arrange the numbers by classifications, for example, gas, basic supplies and home loan, and aggregate each sum. Consider utilizing your Mastercard or bank proclamations to assist you with this. Bank of America customers can use the Spending and Budgeting tool, which automatically sorts your exchanges for easier planning in the portable application or on the web.

Instructions to set up a financial plan

Do you have more than one record? New administrations mean you would now be able to see all your records in a solitary keeping money application.

The initial step to taking control of your funds is completing a financial plan.

It will require a little exertion, but it's an extraordinary method to get a brisk preview of the money you have coming in and going out.

Setting up a spending implies you're:

› Less likely to finish up in debt
› Less likely to get captured out by sudden expenses
› More likely to have a decent FICO assessment
› More likely to be acknowledged for a home loan or advance
› Able to spot areas where you can make reserve funds
› In an incredible position to set something aside for a vacation, another vehicle, or another treat

Plan on setting aside somemoney

Since you've influenced a financial plan, to make an investment funds classification inside it. Endeavor to spare 10 to 15 percent of your pay. If your costs are high to the point that you can't spare that much, it may be an ideal opportunity to curtail. To do as such, identify superfluous items that you can spend less on, for example, amusement and feasting out, and discover approaches to save money on your settled month to month costs.

Tip: Consider the money you put into investment funds a customary cost, like staple goods, to strengthen great reserve funds propensities.

MINIMALISM AND DECLUTTERING

Pick something to put something aside for

Extraordinary compared to other approaches to set aside some money is to set an objective. Begin by considering what you should want to put something aside for— maybe you're getting hitched, arranging an excursion or putting something aside for retirement. At that point make sense of how much money you'll need and to what extent it may take you to spare it. If you have a Bank of America account, you can use the Picture My Goals tool to set up and keep tabs on your development toward your objectives in the portable application.

Here are a few instances of short-and long haul objectives:

Present moment (1– 3 years)

- Emergency finance (3– 9 months of everyday costs, to be safe)
- Vacation
- Down installment for a vehicle

Long haul (4+ years)

- Down installment on a home or a rebuilding venture
- Your tyke's instruction
- Retirement

If you're putting something aside for retirement or your tyke's instruction, consider putting that money into a venture record, for example, an IRA or 529 arrangement. While ventures accompany hazards and can lose money, they also make the open door for exacerbated returns if you plan for an occasion far ahead of time. See step No. 6 for more subtleties.

Take Control of Your Bank Fees
As was the case with your Mastercards, you are most likely also being charged pointless or overinflated bank expenses. ATM expenses, exchange charges, month to month account keeping expenses, and so on. In disengagement, these charges probably won't appear much, but they do all include.

The bank expenses you are paying might just be debatable or at any rate sufficiently adaptable for you to roll out a few improvements.

Stop for a moment to talk with your ledger supervisor and examine how you can potentially rebuild your financial balances and your pulling back propensities to enable you to spare money. They will gladly enable you to out and will furnish you with proposals on how you can lessen these expenses. And obviously, if you're not fulfilled, at that point search around and locate a superior arrangement.

Take Control of Personal Taxes
The vast majority of us set aside charge time for conceded. We pay what we are intended to pay and we only every once in a

MINIMALISM AND DECLUTTERING

long while question regardless of whether we could have saved money.

Stop for a moment to talk with an expense bookkeeper and clarify your circumstance. Educate them that you might want to talk about ideas for making good on less regulatory obligation. Ask them for proposals and direction about what you could use as a duty derivation, and/or how you could potentially spend or put your money so as to decrease the measure of assessment you pay toward the finish of the budgetary year.

Being savvier in the manner in which you handle your charges could potentially spare you thousands of dollars for every year.

Settle on your needs
After your costs and pay, your objectives are likely to have the greatest effect on how you allocate your reserve funds. Make sure to recall long haul objectives—it's essential that making arrangements for retirement doesn't take a secondary lounge to shorter-term needs. Figure out how to organize your funds objectives so you have a reasonable thought of where to begin sparing. For instance, if you realize you will need to supplant your vehicle sooner rather than later, you could begin putting money away for one at this point.

Getting a good deal on Your Car Expenses

Statistically, in the western world, the vast lion's share of individuals possess a vehicle. It could be a vehicle or even potentially a bike or motorbike. Regardless of what sort of vehicle it will be, it's in all probability going to be one of your greatest continuous costs. As it were, it continually empties money from your pocket every week with continuous fuel, upkeep, and protection costs.

It could be contended that a vehicle is an extravagance. It's unquestionably something that many could manage without, but the bother this would cause could potentially risk an individual's salary, for example their capacity to get the chance to work every day. Be that as it may, there are approaches to set aside some money without setting off to the limits and moving your vehicle. How about we investigate these ideas underneath.

Vehicle Maintenance is Paramount

An unmaintained vehicle is just a waste receptacle for money. Adjusting your vehicle routinely will in all likelihood be undeniably more savvy over the long haul than paying for administration and parts when things separate. It's also more secure to drive and conceivably will enable you to dodge unforeseen medicinal costs that emerge from vehicle mishaps that outcome from breakdowns.

MINIMALISM AND DECLUTTERING

Vehicle upkeep also encompasses seemingly insignificant details, for example, ensuring you are driving with the ideal tire weight. When your tires are too level there is more drag and contact with the street, which makes the vehicle's motor work harder, which in this manner consumes more fuel and tosses money down the deplete.

Get a good deal on Insurance

Keeping up your vehicle is clearly critical, but so is protection. Indeed, there are numerous individuals who drive around with no protection inclusion. And truly, they positively set aside some money temporarily. Without any mishaps, they don't have anything to stress over. Be that as it may, what are the assurances?

Vehicle protection gives you genuine feelings of serenity just in case you are engaged with a mishap. Indeed, it will remove money from your pocket that you could have rather used to satisfy your charge cards, or saved into your rainy day account or investment account. In any case, recall that when you're engaged with a mishap "where no doubt about it", you're not just paying for the fix of your own vehicle, but also for the fix of the other vehicle you beat up.

It is, obviously, essential to look for the best protection bargain. Likewise, you can also consult with your present supplier at a superior cost. Potentially you right now have an "Under

25 Driver" alternative for you that adds 20 dollars to your approach every month. Potentially that is something you could manage without. Along these lines, you could potentially spare yourself a couple of hundred dollars for each year. In any case, be mindful so as not to lessen your choices to such a dimension, to the point that you're scarcely canvassed in case of a mishap.

Stay away from These Money Wasting Driving Tendencies

Owning a vehicle is fantastic. It takes you from A to B, in any case, the fuel can also cost you dearly. Nonetheless, there are a few straightforward things you can do that will help make your vehicle unquestionably increasingly prudent and productive.

For example, did you realize that utilizing cooling can diminish the eco-friendliness of your vehicle by up to 10 percent? This is especially valid at lower speeds. It, therefore, bodes well to open a window while driving gradually in suburbia. In any case, at higher rates, the open window can make drag which also brings down the eco-friendliness of your vehicle. In such cases, at higher velocities (on roads) it bodes well to siphon up the cooling instead of opening a window.

You will also consume fuel faster if you drive erratically. By flighty, I mean braking frequently, quickening rapidly, and weaving forcefully all through traffic paths. Pick rather to

MINIMALISM AND DECLUTTERING

back off and relentless your driving. This will assist you with saving fuel costs over the long haul.

Set aside extra money by Being a More Savvy Driver

Here are some further proposals to enable you to save money on fuel costs:

› Avoid driving amid surge hour traffic.
› Use voyage control to smooth out your driving.
› Remove extreme load from your vehicle, especially from the storage compartment.
› Minimize sitting time at traffic lights.
› Consolidate all your errands into one trek.

These are all exceptionally basic and clear ideas. So direct in certainty that it may appear as however these progressions won't make a big deal about a difference, anyway as time goes on you will put more money ideal over into your pocket.

Picking Alternate Transportation Options

Owning a vehicle is costly. Not exclusively are there support costs, protection charges, fuel costs, but there are also enlistment expenses. If you are not kidding about setting aside some money, then you could abandon your vehicle for the present and drive by riding your bicycle or utilizing open transport.

On the other hand, if you like to clutch your vehicle, then you could consider carpooling with a work pal. That way you will potentially slice your fuel costs down the middle through the span of a year.

Pick the correct tools

If you're putting something aside for momentary objectives, consider utilizing these FDIC-guaranteed store accounts:

› Savings account
› Certificate of store (CD), which secures your money for a settled timeframe at a rate that is typically higher than investment accounts

For long haul objectives consider

› FDIC-protected individual retirement accounts (IRAs), which are impose productive bank accounts
› Securities, for example, stocks or common assets. These venture items are accessible through speculation accounts with a merchant. Keep in mind that securities are not protected by the FDIC, are not stores or different commitments of a bank and are not ensured by a bank. They are liable to venture dangers, including the conceivable loss of your vital.

You don't need to pick only one record. Take a gander at all of your choices and consider things like equalization essentials, expenses and loan costs so you can pick the

MINIMALISM AND DECLUTTERING

blend that will enable you to best put something aside for your objectives.

Make sparing programmed

All banks offer computerized exchanges between your checking and investment accounts. You can pick when, how much and where to exchange money or even split your immediate store so a part of each paycheck goes specifically into your bank account. Part your immediate store and setting up mechanized exchanges are straightforward approaches to set aside extra money since you don't need to consider it, and it generally lessens the compulsion to spend the money.

Watch your funds develop

Survey your financial plan and check your advancement consistently. Not exclusively will this assistance you adhere to your own reserve funds plan, but it also causes you identify and settle issues rapidly. These straightforward approaches to spare may even move you to spare more money each day and hit your objectives faster.

Setting aside extra money Around the Home

There are a lot of basic things we can do around the home that can assist us with starting setting aside extramoney. Inside this area we should investigate three noteworthy home-related costs and the small changes we can start making that will keep more money in our pockets.

ALEXANDRA JESSEN

Save money on Your Water Expenses

We use water each day. We clean up, wash stuff, do the dishes, water the garden, use the latrine, cook, and we even beverage this stuff. Given this, water is a major piece of our lives and — except if you're living in the nation — tragically, it's not something we get for nothing from earth.

Figuring out how to deal with the water you use all the more successfully can assist you with saving a lot of moneythrough the span of a year. Consider for example the accompanying water sparing ideas:

> Wash your garments less regularly.
> Reduce the measure of yard watering days.
> Install a keen sprinkler framework.
> Take shorter showers and challenge yourselfto use a clock.
> Avoid cleaning up that typically expend a lot of water.
> Half flush the can rather than the normal full flush.
> Turn off water taps when not being used, for example, while brushing your teeth.

By making these strides you could potentially divide your water utilization costs and therefore potentially spare yourself many dollars every year.

MINIMALISM AND DECLUTTERING

Save money on Your Electricity Expenses

The other significant but vital cost comes as power. In any case, there are a few things you can do to cut your expenses here as well. Here are a few ideas:

› Invest in sufficient protection to keep your home cool During summer and warm During winter. Less warming and cooling required.

› Don't set your warming too high, and your cooling too low. Also, make sure to close your windows.

› Install durable energy-sparing lights around the home.

› Turn off superfluous lights or diminish them to spare power.

› Unplug gadgets and machines that are not being used.

› Use washing machines and dryers During off-crest times. This is for the individuals who are on-crest and off-top power designs.

Moreover, you could, obviously, arrange a superior manage your capacity supplier. If they won't give you a superior arrangement, at that point basically take your business somewhere else.

By making these strides you could potentially spare yourself several dollars for every year on power costs.

Save money on Your Rental Expenses

The third significant cost comes as rental expenses. Leasing a home, level or condo is a transaction. You get what you're ready to arrange. The better arrangement you can arrange the less money you will spend on your living facilities.

You can anyway also spare a lot of lease by livingwith other individuals. Offering your rental costs to others can be a standout amongst the most significant cost-sparing choices you will ever make.

DIFFERENT LEVELS OF MINIMALISM

Minimalism of Desire

This is when you anticipate less from the world. You acknowledge what you have and given things a chance to unfurl without a feeling of privilege. It doesn't mean you quit wanting a superior life. It just methods you let go of the harshness you feel when things don't go your direction.

Minimalism of Possessions

This is when you claim just what you need. You dispose of things that don't serves you and don't purchase things only for owning them. This reaches out to the money you procure. You make the most of it and spend it just on things that will fulfill you and your friends and family and sound. This also implies you don't chase unreasonable measures of money that you don't really need or couldn't in any way, shape or form spend.

Minimalism of Relations

This one's difficult to clarify, coz I don't want you to misunderstand the thought. When you practice minimalism in your relations, you don't gather individuals like social identifications. You quit checking what number of companions you have. On Facebook as well as, in actuality. Because you understand that the measure of people you know doesn't make a difference so much as the nature of the relationship you share with those people. So you keep in your life just the individuals who advance it with their adoration, the individuals who fulfill you and bolster you with all their heart. It's difficult to rehearse this kind of minimalism however, coz if you're not watchful you may turn into a relationship Nazi, who makes a decision about individuals on the value of what they can improve the situation you. This dimension isn't tied in with dismissing all but a select number of individuals. It's tied in with seeing those you invest your energy with for who they genuinely are and ensuring you possess enough energy for the individuals who mean the most to you.

Minimalism of sound

When you practice this sort of minimalism you endeavor to make as little clamor as conceivable. It's about just utilizing the sounds you completely need to. In this way, if you can say something smoothly and unobtrusively, there's no need to shout. If you can move smoothly and gradually, why surge and make a frenzy? This reaches out to minimalism of words, which basically implies you state just what you should to express what is on your mind.

MINIMALISM AND DECLUTTERING

Minimalism of thought
In which you practice care, to lessen over the top reasoning, settle on basic leadership progressively productive and take out pressure and nervousness.

Interest
Those who fall into the curiosity stage may have quite recently found minimalism and the advantages of living with less. At this stage, you're fascinated with the thought and you may end up spending incalculable hours perusing each blog, book, and Facebook page you can discover.

Readiness
At this stage you have discovered you're prepared to roll out the improvement and are presently mentally setting yourself up. You may have started arranging your assets in to heaps and wind up developing increasingly more OK with dividing your things.

Cleansing
Those who fall into the PURGING stage are prepared to start, and may have even felt a jazzed opportunity from hurling their first trash pack loaded up with things. Amid this stage you'll wind up hurling boxes, sacks, and perhaps dumpsters loaded up with things you never again need or have been clutching to be safe. We will in general remain in this phase for some time, and may even come back to it again later on.

Organize

After you've cleansed you start to sort out what remains. During this stage it's tied in with discovering balance in your home and arranging things such that will fill your heart with joy to day life easier.

Avoidance

This stage may happen whenever or after any of the above stages. During this stage we end up becoming exhausted, tired, or baffled with our new lifestyles and we may start to dodge any more advancement. It's critical when you achieve this phase to push through it and spotlight on the positives.

Maintain

After we have cleansed and composed we'll achieve the upkeep organize. Right now we've set up our accepted procedures and it turns out to be second nature to declutter and sort out. Amid this stage you may wind up doing small episodes of cleansing and re-sorting out your space – and that is flawlessly ordinary!

Growth

Your voyage through minimalism will be an extensive one, but it will at last help you to develop. In this stage we've accomplished some type of development and maybe intelligence through our voyage. We can use

MINIMALISM AND DECLUTTERING

this opportunity to spread our insight to other people.

ALEXANDRA JESSEN

WHAT IS THE DOWNSIDE OF MINIMALISM?

People may believe you're unusual at first. It requires investment to teach your loved ones concerning for what reason you're doing things along these lines, and it takes a little mettle to be different. It's totally justified, despite all the trouble. Leo Babauta of mnmlist.com

There are sure malicious aspects at the edge of any essential development, and minimalism is the same. If you fixate on tallying your things or about disposing of all of your stuff or about carrying on with an extraordinary traveling lifestyle, at that point you're overlooking the main issue of minimalism inside and out. Not that it's inappropriate to check your stuff or to venture to the far corners of the planet, it's simply that minimalism isn't about that stuff, it's not tied in with tallying or "deserting everything," and it's absolutely not about fixation. Minimalism is just a tool to get of life's abundance so you can concentrate on life's critical things, things like relations and

MINIMALISM AND DECLUTTERING

seeking after your passions and self-improvement and contributing to others genuinely. Joshua from The Minimalists

As far as I can see, no, there isn't, but I am really new to this! Perhaps the unavoidable actuality a few people don't understand this way and the related decisions, but this isn't so sad. Laura of minimoblog.it

I figure individuals can get too made up for lost time in tallying quantities of things, paring down underneath what's their solace point, and they lose site of why they began the minimalist adventure in any case. Equalization is vital! Robyn Devine of Minimalist Knitter

There are scarcely any drawbacks to minimalism, but at times it's difficult to disclose it to people who have shut personalities. In some cases individuals simply would prefer not to understand minimalism, they see what we're doing and they simply want to contend or expel it as a trend. The greater part of those people are exceptionally joined to their things, and they are hesitant to quit expending because they associate a specific importance with their utilization, they are too appended to a belief system that their stuff brings them satisfaction. Fortunately, after some time, minimalism uncovers all of its favorable circumstances all alone. So if you're tolerant with those people, their brains will open, and they will understand eventually. Ryan from The Minimalists

ALEXANDRA JESSEN

It's an extremely self-uncovering procedure and lifestyle. When we start to expel the diversion and clutter from our life, our brains are obvious to dive further into our very own essence. It tends to be difficult at first as we are compelled to think about our intentions in gathering all this stuff in any case, but it is a decent procedure to great through. It improves us individuals at last. Joshua Becker of Becoming Minimalist

It has been challenging to converse with family and companions about our decision to possess less things. Regularly individuals feel that our different lifestyle decision is an immediate remark without anyone else. To keep discussions light, I generally state this works for us but it's not for everybody. In all actuality I feel that some level of minimalism, scaling back and dismissing commercialization is gainful for everybody. Rachel Jonat of Minimalist Mom

What I've discovered difficult is that numerous individuals respond emphatically — "Minimalism sounds extraordinary! I ought to do that." — but then they remain stuck in stuff. There's a touch of weight, advocating a cause you realize will enhance individuals' lives, if just they would simply participate. Obviously, this is an expectation filled drawback. Anybody can begin whenever. And people do! That is one inspiration that keeps me offering a life of

MINIMALISM AND DECLUTTERING

straightforward living to other people. Dave Bruno from A Guy Named Dave

None! I genuinely can't consider anything. Meg Wolfe of Minimalist Woman

I think the most essential thing to recall is… our identity could really compare to what we call ourselves. Minimalists and hoarders alike, let the emphasis be on how you treat people, and carry on with your life, rather than how much stuff you have or don't have.

ALEXANDRA JESSEN

THE MISTAKES OF MINIMALISM

Minimalism is winding up increasingly more prevalent for an assortment of reasons, especially with the "style de jour" being "easy costly"(as my supervisor has named it), which has some extremely solid minimalism veins going through it and the use of a couple of great created things versus, a rack brimming with shabby clutter. Who knows why the minimalist pattern is blasting – It may be because many individuals feel that lifeoutsidethe house is getting SO riotous that a progressively minimalist structure for the insides will encourage counter that, or perhaps because with the consistently expanding costs on pretty much everything in the stores we think it is presently alright to purchase $400 material cover that is the same as a vintage form that costs an eighth of the cost. Others may lean progressively minimalist essentially because they want to dispose of the stuff they don't need or use – which may also be at fault on the book that I read alongside pretty much every other person "The Life Changing Magic of Tidying Up". Whatever it is, minimalism is slanting.

MINIMALISM AND DECLUTTERING

But minimalism isn't exactly as easy to accomplish as individuals may think. TBH, as somebody who completes a ton of prop styling for their activity "toning it down would be best" in my case, and getting that "simply enough stuff" easy negligible look is quite hard. As a plan strategy, minimalism has been confounded and misused by numerous individuals, as far as I have seen on the web and through a few pictures that are springing up, so we will have a brisk take a gander at the basic errors that people make when they attempt to transform their homes into a minimalist heaven. That is to say, if you will upgrade the look of your home and hurl it all away to kick off said new lifestyle, then you should do it appropriately!

Put Off Starting Because You Don't Like The "Tenets"

One thing that kept me away from beginning with minimalism was my false conviction that it was an "all or nothing" lifestyle. I'd perused a huge amount of blog entries and articles about people who just possessed 100 things or who lived in modest houses and I was fascinated by their lifestyles, but I realized it wasn't for me.

I realized I was continually going to keep some wistful things (old letters, and so forth.) and I liked having a couple of knickknacks. I would not like to live in an all white house and I was never going to get by with only one sets of shoes! I liked living with less but I realized I was never going to be like the general population I read about on the web.

I didn't think minimalism was appropriate for me until the point that I understood ... there's solitary one guideline with minimalism.

Minimalism is tied in with living with goal and being aware of what you allow in your life (things, ideas, individuals, and so forth.).

That is it; there are no other "rules". Minimalism is close to home and what it looks like in your life is dependent upon you. As you long as you're being straightforward with yourself about what adds value or conveys bliss to your life, at that point you're a minimalist. Your adaptation of minimalism probably won't resemble my rendition of minimalism—and that is alright. All things considered, minimalism is a tool to enable you to carry on with a life you adore—not a true objective.

Try Not To Lose Yourself
The web is a unimaginable place to get roused. I personally can say my whole lifestyle has drastically changed, and to improve things, from being propelled by others on the web. I have gone veggie lover, drastically diminished my waste, decluttered the majority of my stuff and set out on a voyage of self value since seeing others do likewise. In any case, I have committed the error en route of losing myself

MINIMALISM AND DECLUTTERING

and my uniqueness. It very well may be easy to simply duplicate what another person is doing and seek it works after you too, but this shockingly doesn't usually work out. We're all totally different, have different existences, have different expectations, wants and needs. We therefore need to each use minimalism (or any lifestyle so far as that is concerned) in different ways. Your adaptation of minimalism will be totally different to mine. Keep in mind that minimalism isn't a challenge. The essentials of minimalism are to relinquish craving and owning stuff to decide your value, and yet when we begin to use minimalism, it very well may entice decide our value based off how little we claim. Try not to allow this to occur, keep your limits and don't lose your identity in the quest for this lifestyle.

Relax

I'm the kind of individual who settles on a choice, clicks my fingers and wants things done straight away. I will in general go for things full power, which can have its advantages and drawbacks. While I had the inspiration to get things sorted out, it wound up disappointing when the truth it wouldn't occur immediately began to rise. I understood I needed to take things easy. I wasn't going to declutter my whole life medium-term. I wouldn't turn a disorganized closet that I had been gathering for the last decade into an insignificant case closet by one week from now. But after some time I understood how mind blowing this time was. I adapted beyond what I would ever have envisioned a straightforward decluttering of my stuff would educate me. During this long procedure of decluttering I was ready to reflect, search inside, understand where I had been, and where I wanted to go. So my recommendation is make things stride by venture such that bodes well for you. Offer yourself a reprieve and relax. Begin with an aspects of your life that is in especially over-burden (for me this was my closet) and go from that point.

Try Not To Make It Unattainable
What is minimalism about? It is to lessen and to just. Minimalism isn't quantified by how little you possess or how white your stylish is. Try not to let it to end up another perfect that you've been sold that you can't satisfy. It needs to stay feasible and comprehensive, as opposed to unattainable and restrictive. Set yourself feasible objectives, for example, clearing all the surfaces in your home, or disposing of a container of things you don't need any longer. There doesn't need to be any limits. Limits just make things farfetched and harder to accomplish. So the main objectives you ought to set for yourself are ones that are inside reach.

Try not to Buy New Stuff
When I originally began decluttering, I gave myself a shopping boycott. Especially when it came to garments. I understood I had all that I

MINIMALISM AND DECLUTTERING

needed, and the impulse to purchase new things needed to be killed. It was a tremendous expectation to learn and adapt for me as for a very long time I generally had a considerable rundown of things I wanted in my closet, my cosmetics sack or whatever. I realized that I needed to relinquish this steady longing for new things and spotlight on sorting out and getting free. The best part is, this procedure did what I trusted it would do and quite a lot more. I never again long to go out on the town to shop, I am more chivalrous than any other time in recent memory when I do need to go out on the town to shop for something, I have turned out to be quite a lot more thankful for all the things I have in my life, and I have spared such a great amount of money simultaneously. So one of the greatest things you can do when you first begin is to instruct yourself to state no to new things. Concentrate on decluttering, limiting and getting free, and discover fulfillment in that (but also don't pummel yourself if you do slip and unintentionally purchase something new, simply proceed onward and gain from it).

Try Not To Put Pressure On Yourself

Don't put weight on yourself. This procedure shouldn't finish up being a distressing one. If you go out and purchase something and think twice about it a short time later, don't thump yourself, simply gain from it! Consider how it affected you and how perhaps you could improve the situation next time. Slip-ups are there to be gained from and if we didn't make them we wouldn't get much of anywhere in our life. Keep in mind that is anything but a goal, but an adventure. Regardless i'm learning regular, committing errors, coming up short and getting back up once more. It is the thing that makes us human, improves us develop and move toward becoming individuals progressing in the direction of our objectives. Relinquish the weight and appreciate the experience!

No Personality
Insignificant DOES NOT EQUAL an absence of identity, but frequently an exposed room is regularly one without simply that. This is a typical mistake in minimalist homes, but running minimalist with your plan doesn't imply that you need to dispose of the sentiment of human nearness and identity in your home. Definitely, keep things straightforward and refined but give yourself some significant craftsmanship, a plant or greenery, a few books that work with your design, and a couple of beautiful (but utilitarian) embellishments.

Doing Without Functionality For Style
Minimalism is, to some degree, about having what you need and nothing more. A few people tragically take this excessively literally. I have done this without anyone else's help, thinking in my mind "this seat is so basic, so refined and so sleek" when in actuality it ought to state "this seat is sufficiently agreeable to sit

MINIMALISM AND DECLUTTERING

on it for .0234 seconds previously you want to move to a different seat". So when choosing your furnishings, stockpiling, or embellishment decisions remember this. Because despite the fact that it might appear to be chic to have a smooth home office that is finished with a reasonable work area, a couple of small adornments and a light, that is REALLY just not handy. You need a considerable amount more as this article appears. Along these lines, if you've stripped things to such a degree, to the point that usefulness has been sacrificed, at that point you've gone too far!

Capacity

Because you are a recently discovered individual from the minimalist mafia doesn't imply that you don't need cautiously thought about capacity. Regardless of who you think you are, or what style or stylistic theme you use, each individual on earth will need a smidgen of capacity, so get yourself a piece that will work for what you need (regardless of whether it is vacant for the principal tad).

Clear Walls

I secured this one a couple of days prior and it does fairly fall under the "No Personality" segment, but it needs calling out once more. I am all for minimalism, but regardless of how refined and insignificant you are, exposed and clear walls will make your space feel chilly, unfilled and generic. Along these lines, in spite of the fact that you probably won't be into a massive gallery wall, think of some as exceptionally very much arranged craftsmanship that works inside your space to bring some life and shading up on those walls of yours.

Shading

I realize you may feel that I supreme HATE shading, but that isn't the case. Indeed, I do veer more towards the tonal and textural sides of things versus implanting things with brilliant hues but it doesn't imply that I loathe it. Especially on account of minimalism, when things may be exceptionally simplified, the case for shading turns out to be significantly increasingly imperative. If you will keep it basic consider injecting some refined shading in to keep the enthusiasm for the room alive.

Terrible Furniture Layout

Many individuals assume that you can't really turn out badly with the format of the furnishings in a minimalist home. All things considered, what amount of furniture can you really have when you take this plan course of "toning it down would be best"? The issue is that the design of your furnishings can in any case appear to be disordered and swarmed; regardless of whether you have not very many things in there and there's a nice measure of room to lay it all out in. Along these lines, when you start to go negligible still remember the customary guidelines of styling and furniture position and don't trade your couch for a thin

MINIMALISM AND DECLUTTERING

lined seat and then two straightforward side seats that may finish of doing the opposite you had proposed for the room.

So whether you are into it or not, simply recollect that negligible doesn't amount to nothing, and basic doesn't mean without identity. Obviously make your home work for you and for each standard there is a reason to break it. Simply don't go out resembling a distinct, tragic space bereft of well... anything. To enable you to begin here are a couple of my most loved insignificant yet beautiful and useful things.

Dispose of The Duplicates

As a Beginner Minimalist bear in mind to dispose of copies. You can alter down somewhat more without agony. Check for things that fill a similar need in your life and alter all but one of them.

What number of sets of boots do you need? Do you need 5 winter coats? What number of angling bars do you need? What number of handbags do you need?

Check the kitchen and carport for copy things to alter down. If you are anything like me, you are a sucker for tools and contraptions. Scale back, lessen, reuse, reuse and reestablish.

This will add to streamlining your life and help you maintain a strategic distance from choice weakness. It can even go far to soothing worry from your life relying upon what number of copy things you claim.

Unfriend and Unfollow The Peanut Gallery

Try not to falter to unfriend and unfollow your minimalist spoilers mentally and now and then physically. We as a whole have counterfeit individuals on our companion's rundown who's continually posting hostile jokes and inadequately explored data. Try not to give false companions a chance to obstruct your advancement. Unfriend them for some time.

Great loved ones can be brutal when they don't understand something. Under the appearance of thinking about you, loved ones can be merciless with analysis, threatening vibe and over association trying to change your conduct to their preferring.

You can't simply unfriend and unfollow great loved ones. They assume a critical job in your life and will dependably be near.

You can unfriend and unfollow them symbolically. Stand solid against this kind of negative conduct should it emerge. Try not to contend and argue your case. Simply grin and proceed with your advancement towards understanding the minimalist lifestyle. When you unfriend and unfollow them symbolically they will take note.

MINIMALISM AND DECLUTTERING

They will also see you are increasingly glad, progressively sorted out, less focused, have progressively extra money and time to make incredible recollections with them. This may stand out enough to be noticed and you may then actually have a savvy discussion about the advantages of carrying on with the minimalist lifestyle.

Making A Decision About Other People

When you finally come to the heart of the matter where you "get" minimalism—you've scaled back your stuff and you've begun to contemplate your life—it's easy to begin making a decision about individuals who aren't minimalists. (Some of the time this isn't deliberate; you're simply amped up for how your life has changed and you can't understand why everybody is ready!)

In any case, purposeful or not, being judgmental is unkind and useless.

I understand your enthusiasm about minimalism, but the most ideal approach to get the message out is to be a positive good example with your own life. Discussion about how minimalism has transformed you and answer questions if they're asked, but don't remark contrarily on other individuals' lives (either to their face or away from plain view). Life is an adventure; we have different ways and we're all at different stages.

Energize, but don't lecture. Move, but don't pass judgment.

Starting Minimalist Keeping Things Just In Case

Keeping Things Just In Case, for what? If you are not utilizing it to dispose of or give it away. Anything that does not increase the value of your life or fulfill you ought to be reexamined.

If it doesn't summon a positive emotion or if you would not promptly supplant it if lost it likely ought to be sold, given or disposed of.

Trust your intuition and not your emotions. If there was a case for the thing it would have happened as of now. In the remote possibility that you disposed of and the thing you currently need, simply use something you officially claim or obtain the thing from another hotspot for that one time use.

As a starting minimalist, you ought to rapidly learn not to emotionally clutch things in the event that something goes wrong. Release those things and release the worry of owning, putting away and overseeing them as well.

MINIMALISM AND DECLUTTERING

CORE PRINCIPLES TO MAXIMIZE LIVING AND LIVE ON PURPOSE

Feeling that what you're doing has a genuine reason and implying that issues to you can have a colossal effect in your life. It makes getting up every day the most energizing thing on the planet. You can hardly wait to begin. Disregard endeavoring to constrain yourself to buckle down, it turns out to be increasingly critical to remind yourself to take breaks to eat!

But how might we develop a progressively important life? The appropriate response is usually confounded. It can rely upon numerous components. I've recorded 10 ideas that I accept will enable you to discover significance in your life consistently, with the goal that you can hardly wait to get up toward the beginning of the day and see what the day will bring.

For what reason do I need to know my qualities?

Qualities give us our feeling of direction. On an authority level, when we line up with our qualities once a day, we have more energy and feel progressively satisfied because we are driving from what's vital to us. When we don't line up with our qualities, we feel less credible and progress toward becoming demotivated about our day by day lives, which reflects in our initiative.

Consider it a tree: values are our foundations that keep us grounded in what's vital to us. The quality of the qualities decides the quality of the storage compartment, branches, leaves and natural product from year to year. A solid tree bolsters the biological community around it; a pioneer with solid qualities underpins the authoritative culture.

How Do I Find My Values?

Qualities are like a compass that guides us toward our "actual north." Let's survey an incredible exercise to help you unmistakably identify your fundamental beliefs. Would you be able to recall a minute where your life couldn't beat that? When everything felt adjusted? It might have even felt like the greatest day of your life. Set aside some opportunity to recall this pinnacle minute and pursue these means:

Portray this pinnacle minute in detail.

If you are chipping away at this activity alone, compose the depiction. If you are doing this activity with somebody, talk about this minute for 2-3 minutes while the other individual takes notes.

MINIMALISM AND DECLUTTERING

Consider and examine what esteems are conspicuous in this specific pinnacle minute.

From the pinnacle minute portrayed above, you could state I esteem:

Being outside

Working with people to build up their potential

Being daring

Pick the esteem or qualities that you've identified as most essential to you.

(Keep in mind that your qualities apply to both your own and expert universes.)

From the three potential qualities I identified above, I pick 'audacious' as the one that is most vital to me in both my vocation and individual life.

Characterize what the picked esteem or qualities intend to YOU.

To me, 'courageous' signifies picking an unusual way, attempting heaps of new things, going to new places (literally and metaphorically), investigating choices and tinkering with ideas to discover arrangements.

Proceed with the procedure until the point that you characterize around 5 fundamental beliefs.

How Do I Put My Values in real life?

Presently it's a great opportunity to incorporate your qualities. Here are three handy tips to enable you to start the procedure.

Seek after Your Passion
I trust everybody should seek after their passion in life. It's what makes life worth living, and gives our lives genuine significance and reason. Each time you take a shot at something you cherish, it makes delight inside you don't like anything else. Figuring out how to use your passions to offer back to the world will give your life extreme significance.

If you can't oversee (or aren't prepared) to chip away at your passion professionally, make certain and set aside a few minutes for it consistently. By chipping away at your passion and turning into a specialist in it, you will eventually have the chance to profit from it. Be prepared to grab that chance!

Pick an esteem name that impacts YOU.
A great many people would name the esteem I identified essentially as "bold". In any case, the word bold doesn't impact me. Rather the name "wind in your face" is substantially more critical for me as a basic belief.

Before settling on a choice, pursue these five stages:
Initially, survey your list of qualities. For this activity, it is best to have your qualities recorded.

MINIMALISM AND DECLUTTERING

At that point ask yourself this inquiry concerning the esteem you have recorded as number one: "On a size of 1 to 10, with 10 being the most astounding, how well does the apparent result of this choice or opportunity line up with esteem number one?" Then record the number.

Ask a similar inquiry regarding each an incentive on your rundown.

After you've appraised the apparent result of this choice or open door for every one of your basic beliefs, include the numbers up and locate the normal.

Lastly, assess the score. Your point is to get a score of seven or higher by and large. If you score beneath seven, the choice or opportunity may not adjust enough to your qualities to be considered.

Check in on your qualities every day
Ideally, you should "check in" on your qualities every day. (If day by day feels like too much, attempt week after week.) Personally, I do this in transit home from work. I ask myself, "How well did my choices and conduct line up with esteem #1 today?" This takes just two minutes yet furnishes you with a decent feeling of what to enhance the following day. It keeps you focused and in contact with what is imperative to you.

Recognize What's Important

Recognize what's vital for you. Record your best 5 things that you accept are the pith of how you want to live. This can incorporate things like "family time," or "sing each day." It could also incorporate increasingly complex ideas, like "genuineness" and "straightforwardness."

Discover a Way to Give Back

Accomplish something that the two distinctions your convictions and passions, while giving something back to the world. By giving something back, we definitely discover reason in the demonstration. By developing a greater amount of these exercises, you will discover your life has additionally significance and reason behind it.

Purposefully help yourself to remember your qualities

It's essential to have a visual notice of your qualities, notwithstanding your rundown of qualities. This keeps them up front in your brain. Here are some easy approaches to help yourself to remember your qualities all the time:

Make a screensaver.

Try not to belittle the intensity of a post-it.

Discover an image that speaks to one of your qualities and keep it somewhere you will see it day by day.

MINIMALISM AND DECLUTTERING

Pick a melody to speak to at least one of your qualities and hear it out once per day as a major aspect of your morning, evening, or night custom.

Simplify Your Life

By simplifying your life, you'll have more opportunity to do what satisfies you and gives your life meaning. It can also help decrease pressure and make your overall life easier to oversee. It can also incredibly enhance your profitability. If you've never attempted to simplify things, it really is an incredible inclination.

Find Your Life's Purpose

If you needed to give yourself a reason to live, what might it be? What might you rely on? What standards do you hold most astounding? Is your life's motivation to help other people? Is it to rouse others with incredible masterpieces, or you words? Finding your life's motivation is an overwhelming task, and when I previously heard the thought, I had no clue where to begin. For techniques on finding your life's motivation, I prescribe Steve Pavlina's blog passages regarding the matter. I also suggest perusing the article What Makes Life Worth Living.

Act naturally Aware

Know about yourself and your activities. Stay aware of what you do consistently, and ensure you are living as per your standards, your life's motivation, and what you are passionate about. Survey your activities every day, considering those that strayed from your way. Work towards revising any occurrences later on. Contemplation is an incredible tool for achieving this task. It causes us increase our mindfulness for the duration of the day.

Focus

Instead of chasing 3 or 4 objectives and gaining next to no ground on them, put all of your energy on a certain something. Focus. Not exclusively will you alleviate a portion of the pressure associated with endeavoring to juggle such a significant number of tasks, you will be considerably more fruitful. Attempt and adjust your objective to something you are passionate about, so that there will be an inborn drive to buckle down and do well.

People More Than Things

Regularly, we are looked with wanting to purchase material merchandise. I prescribe you consider cautiously what you purchase, and think increasingly about spending your cash on experiences with loved ones. Not exclusively will this give further significance to your life by focusing on your connections instead of material riches, but you will be a more joyful individual thus.

Live With Compassion

Both for yourself, as well as other people. Remember the accompanying statement:

MINIMALISM AND DECLUTTERING

"One must be compassionate to one's self before outer compassion" - Dalai Lama

For a few, compassion is the reason for life, what gives it meaning, and what prompts extreme bliss.

Set Daily Goals

In the first part of the, prior day you begin your day, make a list of 3 objectives that you find satisfying and important. Ensure they adhere to your arrangement of standards and convictions. Handle the hardest things first! Try not to make this list too long. By putting too numerous things on the rundown, you'll want to perform various tasks, which isn't great, or you'll feel overpowered, which isn't great either. By endeavoring to do less, you'll wind up accomplishing more.

Doing all of these things on the double may appear to be overwhelming, but you can pick one thing at any given moment and gradually consolidate the ideas into your life. Life is about the voyage, not the goal. Carrying on with a life of direction gives both satisfaction and importance to your adventure.

ALEXANDRA JESSEN

SIMPLICITY OF MINDFULNESS AND MEDITATION

If the basic life really is the best, at that point why so few of us want to live it? I recollect a narrative about a gathering of Mongolian migrants, and the fervor when they purchased their first TV and installed it in their yurt. From that point on, each night, they were transfixed by the TV. No more narrating around the stove, no all the more playing amusements or singing melodies. The TV currently led their recreation time, as it does in such a significant number of households around the globe.

It appears we're hard-wired to search out incitement and multifaceted nature. Truth be told it takes significant control to pick a life of effortlessness, and maybe thus, a life of genuine straightforwardness can frequently turn out to be very inflexible. The straightforward life can also lean towards being oversimplified instead of basic. To imagine there are straightforward answers for our intricate issues is usually gullible – however

MINIMALISM AND DECLUTTERING

engaging. Short, punchy three word trademarks by our pioneers make great nightly news, and can assure the watcher the issue is being dealt with. Later we usually discover that, somewhere off camera, the 'straightforward' arrangement ended up being definitely not, and frequently caused more issues which the cutting edge is currently managing.

However huge numbers of us do long for more noteworthy effortlessness. A withdraw domain offers us the chance to simplify our lives for a couple of days by evacuating a considerable lot of the regular diversions. Rather, we focus on being available in the here and now. Contingent upon the idea of the withdraw, there might be no talking, no perusing, absolutely no browsing Facebook or messages. The structure of the withdraw clarifies where our consideration ought to be – contemplation, eating, strolling, and cleaning the washroom. Toward the finish of retreats, individuals regularly talk about a profound feeling of happiness, of feeling appreciation for basic things like the trees outside the window, the ducklings they viewed amid a break, the delicate endeavors of the cooks. After some time, if we go to standard withdraws and think each day, a portion of that happiness and appreciation tends to saturate our every day lives.

ALEXANDRA JESSEN

The Art of Simplicity – Straightforwardness

In a fast paced occupied existence where consistently gets immediately loaded up with movement and finishing a 'plan for the day' it's easy to disregard the straightforward delight of 'simply sitting' in contemplation and the advantages it can convey to your life. Too frequently we get focused on chasing our tails getting it done, family and different duties, contemplation at that point is a Time Out of the monotonous routine of seeking after our objectives and allows the space for stillness to develop and an opportunity to recollect the straightforwardness of simply being.

Contemplation can turn into a quest for unattainable objectives of preeminent edification or relative flawlessness but by simply sitting and simply breathing there are no more desires or needing for any splendid experience, reflection would then be able to end up the statement of straightforwardness or as Zen Master Dogen educated – simply sitting is simply the outflow of illumination without whatever else included.

Maybe this is something we have lost in our cutting edge world, the capacity to simply sit still and be content. Without attempting to accomplish something or always enhance ourselves we can allow straightforwardness to rise naturally. This is something unfamiliar to

MINIMALISM AND DECLUTTERING

us but it blends an old notice of the delight of simply being.

I have discovered the contemplation directions from a Tibetan knowledge convention called Mahamudra probably the most significant I have ever run over and it's the effortlessness of the guidelines that is accurately its splendor. Mahamudra is discovering harmony and stillness by giving the mind a chance to be as it is without controlling it or attempting to transform anything; the consciousness of things ideal similarly as they are. Its an acknowledgment that things similarly as they are correct currently have a specific stunner to them regardless of how disordered or untidy everything may appear.

Giving the mind a chance to be similarly as it is, at that point basically sit still and essentially breath and the delight of straightforwardness and genuineness easily emerges. Without constraining anything simply unwind and see the effortlessness of being in the now. The renowned Chinese Philosopher Confucius says:

When we consider contemplation, numerous pictures ring a bell. There may even be sure stigmas associated with it. Usually saw as religion-based or as "another age" convention, with yogis roosted in the lotus position reciting Ohm for quite a long time.

In truth, there are numerous approaches to characterize reflection. But it can also be inspected from a non-denominational, target focal point. Its training doesn't need to be convoluted or grandiose. Contemplation can just be tied in with being still and quiet. It very well may focus on breath. It tends to be the specialty of quieting our brains.

"Life is really basic, but we demand making it muddled."

In the present current culture, contemplation can be a profitable tool with a large group of advantages. There is a plenitude of writing about its exceptional advantages. For example, its training has been known to alleviate pressure, stress, uneasiness and sorrow. It can help construct confidence and mindfulness. It can even battle a wide assortment of ailments. Pinto includes, "And the best part is that there are positively no unfavorable symptoms. I imagine that nowadays, we as a whole realize that a positive perspective has a solid positive effect on one's wellbeing, connections, and occupation."

To put it plainly, contemplation can enhance our lives. Our timetables are over-stuffed and we want to top off every minute. We get occupied. We fixate on the past and worry about what's to come. Contemplation recommends that when you sit in stillness, our outlook can be changed. We are established

MINIMALISM AND DECLUTTERING

right now. From that point, we can get away from the continuous racket of our psyche and look at things in a progressively target way.

Its training can be valuable for the entire family. Reflection instructors concur that children can also receive its rewards. "Kids are naturals when it comes to thinking because they have a characteristic affinity for bliss, and for looking for their own joy," clarifies Pinto.

At the end of the day, reflection ought to be polished in a cheerful and straightforward way. If you might want to start a contemplation practice in your family, begin with the basics. The thought is to enjoy a reprieve from your bustling life and cut out some holy time. There are contemplation classes, books and recordings to rouse you. See what impacts you and consolidate that into your life. Keep a receptive outlook and see what benefits contemplation can convey to your whole family.

I think the specialty of straightforwardness is allowing things to be without control or manufacture – euphoria and harmony can be found whenever you want to stop, be still and simply take some cognizant breaths. This is the Way of reflection and figuring out how to appreciate the basic things in life is really a gift.

To have the capacity to relish some tea, appreciate gazing toward the sky or simply grinning to yourself about being alive is magnificently basic and at the some time totally fulfilling. Keeping it straightforward is keeping it genuine. Effortlessness also infers a capacity to not need to intellectually clarify each and every thing that occurs but rather to acknowledge things as they are with a feeling of transparency and riddle.

It is something that must be experienced instead of discussed, and regularly to state the words 'I don't have a clue' is the start of unwinding into a honest straightforwardness. Effortlessness is constantly accessible when you set aside the opportunity to see the sheer receptiveness of the present minute.

30-DAY MINIMALISM CHALLENGE

For this post, I've gathered 30 one-day assignments to enable you to plunge your toes into minimalist living, find loads of new things about yourself and get a major head begin. If you want to carry on with a more straightforward, progressively deliberate life with less stuff but additional time and energy for the general population and things you adore, make January your period of progress!

The standards for the challenge: Do one assignment consistently, the request is your call. Try not to avoid multi day. That is it.

Stay disconnected for one day

Web based life, interminable news streams and articles all deplete our energy and keep us in a steady occupied state. So today: Log off and appreciate the serenity of remaining separated.

Relinquish an objective

The way to accomplishing objectives as a minimalist is to set the correct ones in any case! Rather than chasing things you figure you should want, make sense of what might really satisfy you. Relinquish any objectives that aren't important to you for good today.

Identify your 3-6 principle needs

Most importantly, minimalism is tied in with making sense of what is important most to you in life and how to add a greater amount of that to your everyday daily schedule. Today: Dig profound and make a list of your 3-6 top needs in life.

Pursue a wake-up routine

Begin your day with an unwinding and empowering wake-up routine, rather than promptly browsing your email or online networking encourages. Reflect, compose, do yoga or read a book.

Streamline your perusing list

Today: Downsize your perusing list, withdraw and expel bookmarks. Keep just sources that are significant to you and that add something to your day.

Figure out how to appreciate isolation

Go through somewhere around 3 hours (ideally progressively) alone, without online networking or foundation prattle from the TV. Focus on what it feels like to be in total isolation and, if you like, record your contemplations.

Cut back your excellence gathering

Handle your magnificence items today! Compose a list of all that you use all the time

MINIMALISM AND DECLUTTERING

from the highest point of your head (without checking your magnificence cupboards). Discard out or give everything else.

Kill notifications

Email and online life notifications make for an exceptionally responsive work process. Only for now: Turn off all notifications and check your feeds just at assigned occasions.

Assess your responsibilities

Record all of your customary responsibilities, for example enrollments, side ventures and different obligations. At that point be straightforward: Which of these do you just keep up out of commitment and which do you really appreciate or are important to you?

Characterize your objectives during the current year

Defining objectives shields you from living in a receptive, passive manner and causes you adjust your every day activities to your actual needs. Today, put aside something like thirty minutes to choose 1-3 major, energizing objectives during the current year.

Take care of your personal business

Hold a full evening to experience your closet piece-by-piece and dispose of whatever doesn't make you feel certain and propelled. Look at this exercise manual if you have an inclination that your closet could use a patch up.

Make a stride towards taking in another expertise
Learning expands your frame of reference and can be so much fun! Today, pick an expertise you have dependably been interested about, accumulate whatever you need and begin!

Look at your day by day propensities
Today, investigate your regular propensities, from your morning schedule to the manner in which you work to your night exercises. Which propensities might you be able to enhance, which would it be advisable for you to drop, which new ones might you be able to get?

Ruminate for fifteen minutes
Contemplation diminishes pressure and nervousness and gives you a huge amount of additional energy and mental lucidity. Use an application like Headspace to try it out today.

Declutter your computerized life
Deal with your advanced clutter today: Spring-clean your work area, erase any documents you needn't bother with any longer and set up a basic, simple envelope structure.

No-objection day
Griping is never beneficial and an impetus for negative idea designs. Challenge yourself to not gripe about small stuff today. Either acknowledge the circumstance and proceed onward, or discover an answer.

MINIMALISM AND DECLUTTERING

No email or web based life until lunch

Use your most profitable hours of the day to complete poo and oppose checking your feeds until the point when noon. At that point commend the amount more you achieved!

Try not to purchase anything for 24 hours

Leap forward an undesirable cycle of emotional spending by going on a one-day shopping fast. Try not to purchase anything, not in any case nourishment or basics, for 24 hours (ensure you prepare ahead of time). At that point perceive how you feel!

Practice single-tasking

Nothing channels energy faster than always exchanging between numerous tasks. Practice really focusing on one thing at any given moment utilizing a clock like this one. Stick to short blasts of concentrated work with standard breaks in the middle.

Unfollow and unfriend

De-stretch your web based life experience by being somewhat more specific about who you pursue. Do you really need to remain Facebook companions with people you haven't addressed in years? Experience your list and scale down.

Go for a walk and practice care

Strolls are an incredible chance to rehearse care. Pick a recognizable course and give careful consideration to your surroundings with all detects. You'll be astonished what number of new things you'll notice and how invigorated you'll feel after.

No TV all day, read

All electronic gadgets emanate a blue light that irritates our melatonin generation and decreases rest quality. Along these lines, rather than completion your night with a few scenes of your most loved show, snuggle up on the lounge chair with a decent book today!

Diary for twenty minutes

Composing causes you arrange your contemplations and de-stresses. Take a seat for twenty minutes today to expound on whatever rings a bell. If you like it, consider consolidating a speedy day by day composing session into your customary everyday practice.

Make a loosening up sleep time schedule

Enhance your rest quality and energy levels by setting aside the opportunity to legitimately slow down toward the finish of every day. Do some composition, read a decent book, have some tea, prepare everything for the following day, and so forth. Attempt it today!

Go unabashed

Re-set what you consider fundamental by following a stripped down magnificence routine only for now (no make up and negligible healthy skin). You may well find that huge numbers of the items you thought you need are really discretionary and would then be able to streamline your standard schedule a bit.

Practice appreciation

Turning into a minimalist is most importantly about being careful and valuing the little (and huge) things that are now a piece of your life. Assignment for now: Write a not insignificant rundown of everything (and everybody) you are appreciative for in life.

Leave an entire day impromptu

In our way of life, we are so used to making the most out of each free moment of the day, it very well may be relatively unnerving to not have any plans for once. Be bold today and see where it takes you.

Identify your pressure triggers

The initial move towards lessening regular pressure is to pinpoint your own triggers. Attempt this: Take notes of your feelings of anxiety and your exercises at normal interims all through a weekday. When you have identified your pressure triggers, make sense of how you could avert or balance them later on.

Get out your garbage cabinet

Disposing of clutter can have a relatively remedial impact, because it encourages you manage all of the different emotions that are appended to your stuff. Finish your own treatment session today by clearing out the most cluttered cabinet/box/corner of your house.

Assess your last five purchases

Growing progressively moral and less consumerist ways of managing money is critical to carrying on with a less difficult life. Today, assess your last five trivial purchases. How useful did they end up being and how might you enhance your purchasing choices later on?

MINIMALISM AND DECLUTTERING

TIPS TO DECLUTTER YOUR HOME

When you've managed the emotional reasons you can begin to get breaking! Here's 10 tips for decluttering:

Use a 'maybes' heap.
Rather than obsessing about a few things, have a 'maybes' heap and come back to it later and manage them all in one go.

Work rapidly
don't spend an excessively long time umming and ahhing over what to keep. Your gut drive is usually right. If in uncertainty – ask yourself when you 'genuineness' last used the thing – if it's more than 1 season back then receptacle it!

Pass on the pleasure.
If something has given you pleasure in the past but you believe you most likely won't use it again – pass on that pleasure. Envision how incredible it will be to give that experience to another person.

Discover 'places' for things.
Settle on a place for things like your keys, sunglasses or wallet. Stick to it and you'll never lose another thing again!

Try not to consider it too important!
Try not to think about this as a major errand rather choose to have some good times with it. Wrench up the stereo with your most loved tunes and chime in while you declutter.

Help other people less blessed than you.
Consider decluttering a beneficent demonstration. You can give away things that you never again need to the individuals who truly are in need. When we take the focus off ourselves and onto others it prevents us from fixating on insignificant things.

Sort things into 4 expansive heaps
the primary area to toss out, the second segment for philanthropy, the third segment to offer and the fourth segment to keep.

Set yourself an objective or a due date.
Defining objectives makes inspiration and energy so you can dedicate yourself completely to the task. If you need some assistance with defining objectives read 8 Tips for defining objectives.

Focus on the result.
Picture how stunning your home will look when you're set. Have a reasonable picture of

MINIMALISM AND DECLUTTERING

what you want it to resemble – and continue alluding back to this to prop you up!

ALEXANDRA JESSEN

DECLUTTERING: PRACTICAL STEPS FOR LIVING WITH LESS

Begin easy. "Your initial phase the correct way does not need to be a major one. Our own adventure started by expelling the clutter from our vehicles. Literally. The primary things we limited were ketchup parcels, Happy Meal toys, old receipts, and seldom used music CDs. It wasn't huge, but it made us move the correct way.

"Our next tasks incorporated the family room, the room, and our closet. Each room or storage room was somewhat harder than the past. But we found vital force in the early strides to help bring us through the difficult ones not far off," Becker said.

Pick a lived-in region to start. "When you initially start to declutter your home, pick a zone that is frequently used. There are numerous advantages to owning less - clear, open spaces with less diversions is truly outstanding. As you evacuate clutter, you will rapidly experience them.

MINIMALISM AND DECLUTTERING

"And the most ideal approach to completely understand these advantages is to start decluttering a room that is used frequently. This could be a family room, a room, an office, or a restroom. Begin decluttering in an easy, lived-in zone. You'll cherish it. And find increased inspiration," Becker said.

Contact each thing. "Your decluttering venture isn't a race. It took a very long time to aggregate all the clutter in your home and it will take in excess of an evening or end of the week to evacuate it. My very own group of four took nine months. You will love taking as much time as is needed. And you will love requiring the additional push to physically contact each thing in your home.

"Physically handling every thing powers our brains to settle on purposeful choices about them. In the wake of contacting every thing, put it in one of three heaps: keep, migrate, or expel. From that point, handle quickly. And then rehash," Becker said.

Incline toward giving over moving. "You can make more cash by moving your unneeded clutter. And if you really need the cash, take the plunge. There are endless sites that can help. But know that endeavoring to move your clutter is tedious, bulky, and regularly adds to the worry of decluttering.

"If cash isn't a prompt worry for your family, move your significant things on Ebay, but give everything else to a nearby philanthropy. You will discover delight and satisfaction in liberality - and that experience will be imperative going ahead as you try to conquer the device of commercialization," Becker said.

Peruse a book. "The primary book I read on decluttering was Clear Your Clutter with Feng Shui by Karen Kingston. While feng shui never turned into a core value in my home, the musings in the book were useful for our adventure. It is essential to be reminded that others battle with a similar issue. And it is gainful to hear new answers for these issues.

"The book was great, regardless I suggest it. But I also prescribe Simplify,Organised Simplicity, The Joy of Less, and The Life-Changing Magic of Tidying Up. Any of them will be useful and persuading," Becker said.

Tell a companion. "Satisfaction is most satisfying when it is imparted to other people. Recount your anecdote about your goals to declutter. You will discover individuals are eager to attempt it themselves. They will support you. They will rouse you by considering you responsible and ask you how things are going whenever you see them.

"As an extra advantage, when you share your story, you will be helped again to remember the reasons you chose to declutter in any case," Becker said.

MINIMALISM AND DECLUTTERING

Approve of blemish. "Try not to give ideal a chance to wind up the adversary of better. The first occasion when you experience your home, you won't expel all the clutter. You'll keep stuff that didn't need to be kept. You'll see it too difficult to part with a few things. You may even evacuate some things you'll finish up wishing you had kept," Becker said.

ALEXANDRA JESSEN

TECHNIQUES FOR PRACTICAL DECLUTTERING

There isn't one right approach to declutter, but much of the time, the dispose of everything medium-term strategy isn't practical. Consider the enormous changes you've made in your life.

Play the memory diversion.
If you keep things away, you've likely composed the substance outwardly of each crate. Something else, how might you realize what was inside? Recollecting what's in the crate without a mark is a genuine trial of how vital the stuff is to you. Fill a crate with things you aren't exactly prepared to part with, but aren't sure you really need. Stamp the case "give following 30 days." Then move the case outside of anyone's ability to see, marked. "Give if I needn't bother with." After 30 days, if you can't recollect what's in the crate or don't miss the substance, give it all without opening.

MINIMALISM AND DECLUTTERING

Welcome everybody to the gathering.

When you start decluttering, welcome your family to participate. Try not to drive, welcome. Keep in mind, however, that while the easiest place to search for clutter is in another person's space, your family may dislike the weight. Along these lines, begin with your very own things. Give relatives a chance to take a shot at decluttering their own things at their very own pace. If you want people to see the delight in less, live happily with less yourself.

Set the stage.

Challenge yourself and your family to three months of just purchasing the basics and/or disposing of something whenever another thing comes into your home. Approaching things incorporate purchases, gifts, and items from school or the workplace. At the end of the day, everything checks. If you purchase another match of shoes, give an old combine. If you purchase another restorative item, hurl the leftovers of old ones that are presumably terminated at any rate. If you purchase new wine glasses, give the ones you were utilizing previously. This will help anticipate clutter creep while you are decluttering.

Obviously characterize the mission.

There is a major difference among arranging and decluttering. Sorting out methods you're simply moving stuff starting with one place then onto the next. Rather than buckling down to locate the ideal spot for something, perceive that it probably won't have a place in your home or your heart at all any longer.

Declutter In Stages.

Begin with the easy stuff to construct your decluttering muscles. Things, for example, copies, embellishing things, kitchen hardware you haven't used in years, things you don't use or appreciate, and things away that haven't been a piece of your life for quite a while will be easier to release. Every thing you let go of will give you the quality and inspiration to relinquish the following.

Excursion Light.

Apply your decluttering procedures when you travel, and help up your suitcase. Pressing softly is an incredible practice for living delicately. On your next trek, pack for a large portion of the length of your get-away. Leave the "to be safe" things at home, and notice how light you feel when strolling through the air terminal, unloading at the inn, and investigating another area without stressing over all of your stuff.

Relinquish your emotions too.

When you let go of things that you've clutched because you spent too much cash to get them or influenced a significant venture on them, to endeavor to also relinquish the blame of terrible purchasing choices and overspending. If you battle with blame about giving up, hanging tight, cash spent, or time wasted, it's an ideal opportunity to shift each liable idea to one of appreciation. If you are considering, "I shouldn't have spent that cash," exchange your idea for "I'm appreciative that I perceive what's most essential to me now."

You have effectively sufficiently paid. If you don't relinquish the blame, you will keep on paying with your time, consideration, energy, and heart. The genuine expense of the things you are holding is a lot higher than the numbers on the sticker price.

Ask For Help.
Some of the time, we are so connected to our stuff that it's difficult to realize when to hang on and when to give up. Ask a companion or relative to encourage you. Give this individual a chance to cast a ballot "yes" or "no" to dress, beautiful pieces, and different things. Far and away superior, swap administrations, and consent to go to your companion's home beside respond.

Reconsider wistfulness.
The last phase of decluttering is usually put something aside for the all the more challenging things, including the costly and nostalgic stuff. If the costly things have no significance or reason in your life, move them, and use the returns to settle debt or give to philanthropy.

If you are sparing things to pass down to your youngsters, think about that they most likely don't want it. A Washington Post article called "Stuff it: Millennials Nix their Parent's Treasures" paints a convincing picture for guardians who are hanging on: "As people born after WW2, conceived somewhere in the range of 1946 and 1964, begin wiping out upper rooms and basements, many are finding that twenty to thirty year olds, conceived somewhere in the range of 1980 and 2000, are not all that keen on the lifestyle trappings or nostalgic memorabilia they were so affectionately raised with. Scaling back specialists and expert coordinators are encouraging guardians whose youngsters seem to have lost any wistful connection to their lovable child shoes and family treasure quilts." at the end of the day, your child's don't want your stuff, so you can relinquish it now.

Your kids realize genuine treasures are not in the loft or contained in any physical thing.

Account for additional.
Decluttering starts when you want less; less clutter, less debt, and less diversions, but eventually, you'll begin to want more. Prepare for a greater amount of what you really want from your life, space for how you want to contribute to the world, and space for what makes a difference to your heart. Account for a greater amount of the well done.

Each of these gradual systems for handy decluttering will enable you to make more space, time, and love effortlessly rather than battle, and bliss rather than despair. Be thoughtful to yourself and to your family as you figure out how to relinquish the clutter, and clutch the affection.

ALEXANDRA JESSEN

HOW TO START DECLUTTERING YOUR LIFE: 5 SIMPLE STEPS

How to Declutter

"It's anything but an every day increase, but a day by day decrease. Hack away at the inessentials."

Bruce Lee

I cherish decluttering.

Why?

Because a life with less clutter makes it easier to:

Lessen the day by day stress and find inward harmony.

Focus and to complete a superior occupation (and frequently do it snappier too).

Keep your consideration consistently on what is most imperative and important in life.

MINIMALISM AND DECLUTTERING

Clutter makes diversion. It can make pressure and disarray that you may not know that it's making.

But after you have decluttered there is usually a vibe of feeling more quiet and lighter, more cheery and having the capacity to think all the more plainly.

Decluttering a cabinet, rack or some sort of room in your life can be a surprisingly positive experience not simply practically. But for you as an individual both emotionally and mentally.

This is the most imperative reason why I declutter.

But it, obviously, also opens up space. It can push you to at times procure a touch of additional cash. It can make another person more joyful by giving them something you have no use for any longer.

If you have only 5 or 10 minutes to save today and want to venture out simplify your external and internal life then I suggest uncluttering only one small space in your house.

Here's the manner by which I declutter in five speedy advances.

Pick a cabinet or a rack. Void it out and get it out. Put everything that was in that space in one major heap.

ALEXANDRA JESSEN

Settle on decisions about those things, each one in turn. For every thing in that heap ask yourself this: have I used this in the past year? If not, at that point usually quite safe to state that you won't use it later on either.

Give it away or trash it? If you are not keeping it then you might want to offer it to somebody you realize that you think could make great use of it. Or then again you can give it away to your neighborhood philanthropy. If that is the case placed it in a crate or sack for that reason. And if you simply want to trash it then put it at that point place it in a sack where you'll gather the trash things amid this brief uncluttering session.

If you are keeping it, at that point locate a home for it. It could be at one of the front corners of your cabinet or to one side in the best retire of your bookcase. Having a home for every thing where you set it back each time subsequent to utilizing it will diminish the week by week clutter in your home and you will dependably have the capacity to easily discover the thing.

If you are uncertain about the thing at that point place it in a 6-month box. Put that case away somewhere where you can easily get to it – a wardrobe for instance – if you need something from it. Outwardly of the container compose the date when you put the stuff in it. a half year later get the case and see what is still in it. If you haven't used those things in the

MINIMALISM AND DECLUTTERING

past a half year then you have no need for them and you can securely give them away or toss them out.

By making small 5-10 minute strides when you have some an opportunity to save you can declutter a ton over fourteen days.

Or then again that first small advance may lead you to uncluttering an entire room without a moment's delay. Or on the other hand rouse you to take 5-10 minutes tomorrow to begin decluttering your work space.

ALEXANDRA JESSEN

HERE'S HOW TO MAKE MINIMALISM WORK FOR YOU

It's likely not a stretch to state that you have a ton of stuff you needn't bother with. Regardless of whether you endeavor to remain over clutter and you're truly great at keeping everything perfect and clean, you could stand to scale it back a bit – everybody could. But we've all turned out to be so used to amassing things and utilizing them as a measure of our prosperity, that disposing of all that appears to be a stage in reverse. However, minimalists have figured out how to do only that.

The minimalism lifestyle has been picking up steam throughout the previous couple of years and it is by all accounts achieving a point where the vast majority in any event think about it. Why? Because it's sort of fascinating to perceive how people who live in modest houses figure out how to benefit as much as possible from each and every inch of room or how liberating it is to live with less.

MINIMALISM AND DECLUTTERING

There are a lot of books on minimalism if you're keen on perusing up on it, but probably the best ones incorporate The Life-Changing Magic of Tidying Up: The Japanese Art of Decluttering and Organizing by Maria Kondo, Minimalism: Live a Meaningful Life by Joshua Fields Millburn, The Joy of Less by Francine Jay and Everything That Remains: A Memoir by the Minimalists by Joshua Fields Millburn and Ryan Nicodemus. All four present the masters of carrying on with a life less confused by things and all the more loaded with experiences. Or on the other hand you could simply watch the narrative on Netflix!

You might not want to go to boundaries to wind up a genuine minimalist, but that doesn't mean there aren't some minimalist standards you can't matter to your life to some degree. It's all about parity. Here are a couple of ways you can consolidate minimalism into your life without surrendering all that you possess.

Begin small
Discarding or giving all that you possess in one day isn't likely to be an extraordinary thought. Rather, you need to begin with one zone of your home, like your kitchen for instance. Do you have a group of old dishes that you never use but you're keeping on hand "in the event of some unforeseen issue"? Possibly it's an ideal opportunity to give them away. Because it's not useful to you any longer doesn't mean another person won't esteem it.

Hastily discarding everything is anything but a genuine answer for your clutter issue. You must be attentive and deliberate about what you want to keep and what you want to dispose of, or else you won't bring an end to any negative behavior patterns and you'll simply supplant it all with new stuff. To begin, attempt the 30 Day Minimalism Game

Dark colored Wooden Book Shelf
If you took a gander at your closet truly, what level of the apparel you claim would you say you have worn in the last 3 months? Shouldn't something be said about the last a half year, or the last year? If you have things that never wear, for what reason would you say you are keeping them? It's another case of accumulating things "in the event that something goes wrong" you may need them one day. But the thing is, you wouldn't wear that dark dress again because you either don't love it any longer or it doesn't fit, which is the reason you've just worn it once at any rate.

It may sound amusing, but the less garments you have, the less time you'll spend griping that you don't have anything to wear. Keep your closet basic and you'll never have an issue assembling an outfit, last moment or not.

Pinpoint the things that satisfy you
Being a minimalist isn't about just having things that are significant. You can and ought to have a couple of things that really fulfill you

MINIMALISM AND DECLUTTERING

regardless of whether they aren't really down to earth. If you want to peruse, it's alright to have a book gathering. If music is your passion, don't dispose of your phonograph and guitar because you don't use them consistently. You're ought to have assets that really speak to your identity as long as they bring you joy. The key is to know precisely what fulfills you so you're OK with letting everything else go.

Investigate your ways of managing money

What you burn through cash on is a decent marker of what you consider "necessities". Do you go out to eat a great deal? It is safe to say that you are an impulsive customer who purchases things that are at a bargain regardless of whether you needn't bother with them? Do you adhere to a financial plan, or simply spend and seek after the best? Limit the vulnerability in your spending and you'll finish up with less random purchases that you don't actually need. If you find that you frequently purchase things as an approach to perk yourself up, it may be an ideal opportunity to locate another approach to diminish pressure.

ALEXANDRA JESSEN

CONCLUSION

Minimalism has become a popular word in the last 10 years but it is so much more than that. As consumerism takes a choke hold over people, some have chosen to take a step back and see what really matters in their lives.

Minimalism is about remaining happy and content while having less. We will show you how other people have walked away from the hype of consumerism.

The prospect of living with less clutter is speaking to many, and the advantages are outstanding. Owning less stuff implies possessing more energy for the most essential aspects of our lives, and even feeling progressively good in our own home. As alluring as those outcomes might be, the prospect of decluttering a home can be overpowering with a lifetime of stuff gathered in basements and storage rooms.

While limiting will likely require significant time and exertion, having a decent decluttering strategy to pursue can have a significant effect.

It wasn't until Amy and I discovered a decluttering strategy called The Minimalist

MINIMALISM AND DECLUTTERING

Game that we began gaining predictable ground towards disposing of the clutter in our lives.

Whichever decluttering strategy you pick, it's most essential that you just begin. Life improves past the consistent worry of clutter, it just takes some time and exertion to arrive.

Life is intended to be experienced, not passively anticipated through the screens that encompass us once a day. It may sound threatening, but there are really just a couple general ideas you need to keep mind. So whether you're keen on exchanging your marketed lifestyle for finish straightforwardness, executing a few tips to help you serenely live with less, or just decluttering your condition for increased association and decreased pressure, these small tips will undoubtedly set you on course for progress - all without making too much disturbance your day by day schedule.

Simply ahead and begin living spotless, light and free, no bargains!

Minimalism will appear to be unique for everybody, and it doesn't mean you can't have a house, vehicle or occupation.

It's tied in with decluttering yourself from material belongings and freeing your life of stays.

Minimalism is the tool that allows you to focus on just the vital things. It allows you to carry on with your life all the more intentionally and with significance.

Minimalism is a lifestyle, it's a voyage that takes every day focus and duty to enhancement. Making small, day by day upgrades is critical.

I hope this book was able to help you to get clear idea about minimalism & decluttering. Thanks for reading the book.

www.ingramcontent.com/pod-product-compliance
Lightning Source LLC
Chambersburg PA
CBHW070042230426
43661CB00005B/727